THE

NHL

Today's Stars
Tomorrow's Legends

THE
NHL

Today's Stars
Tomorrow's Legends

James Duplacey and Mark Paddock

Photography by Bruce Bennett Studios

JG PRESS

Published in the USA 1997 by JG Press
Distributed by World Publications, Inc.

The JG Press imprint is a trademark of
JG Press, Inc.
455 Somerset Avenue
North Dighton, MA 02764

Produced by
Brompton Books Corp.
15 Sherwood Place
Greenwich, Connecticut 06830

ISBN 1-57215-237-0

Printed in China

Page 1: Pavel Bure's virtuosity actually cost him a berth on the NHL's All-Rookie Team. During his freshman campaign of 1991-92, Bure played both left wing and right wing with equal flair, and by doing so, actually split his own vote. As a result, he became the only Calder Trophy winner not to be selected to the all-freshman squad.

Page 2: Joe Sakic, who led all post-season scorers in goals (18) and points (34) during the 1995-96 playoffs, lifts the Stanley Cup high above his head in what has become a traditional championship salute.

Page 3: The slick-skating Teemu Selanne reached the 100-point plateau for the third time in his career during the 1996-97 season, compiling a team-high 109 points for the Mighty Ducks of Anaheim.

Below: Although the Great One struggled through a mid-season scoring slump in 1996-97, he proved he hadn't lost his delicate touch by setting up 72 goals during the campaign, tying him with Mario Lemieux for the NHL lead.

Contents

Introduction

To many hockey pundits, the 25-year period between 1942 and 1967 has long been considered the "golden age" of hockey; and while it's true that many of the game's greatest names plied their trade during that quarter-century, when historians look back at the years between 1980 and 2000 they will recognize it as the sport's second golden age. It is a period that gave the hockey world Wayne Gretzky, hockey's greatest ambassador and the man who rewrote the NHL record book, and still owns or shares over 60 individual scoring records, many of which may never be touched. When the Great One was traded from Edmonton to Los Angeles in 1988, the move immediately gave the game a higher profile in the United States. Before the deal, there were only four leagues and 32 cities in the United States that featured professional hockey. Today, there are nine pro leagues operating in 105 U.S. cities and the number is still growing. The advent of in-line skates and the success of roller hockey have created a passion for ice hockey in areas where the game had little or no exposure previously. The opening of the European market in the 1970s and Russian frontier in 1989 has made hockey one of the world's true global sports.

But of course, all this would not be possible if the on-ice product did not feature some of the greatest talents ever to strap on the blades. Of the 46 NHL players who have reached the 1,000-point plateau, 34 accomplished the feat after 1980 and 18 of these superstars are still active, and still producing as the 1997-98 season begins. Although some of the game's aging veterans will soon be moving on, their lengthy list of achievements is already the stuff of legend. Wayne Gretzky has dominated his sport like no other athlete. In his early years with the free-wheeling Oilers, the Great One was a scoring machine. He set a

Opposite left: When he finally surpassed the last of Gordie Howe's scoring marks during the 1993-94 season, Wayne Gretzky said there were only two other milestones he would like to reach before he retired: 3000 career points and 1847 assists.

Opposite right: Patrick Roy proved he was a step above any other netminder during the 1992-93 playoffs by winning an NHL record 10 overtime games in a row.

Right: With a pair of Stanley Cup titles and an NHL scoring crown already to his credit, Jaromir Jagr appears ready to assume the throne vacated by Mario Lemieux in 1997.

Below: Before he even played a game in the NHL, Eric Lindros already had a Memorial Cup ring, a World Junior Championship gold medal and a Canada Cup championship to his credit. Even his detractors agree that a Stanley Cup title will soon be his "Next One."

new standard with 50 goals in 39 games and became the first – and only – player to score over 90 goals in a season when he slipped 92 pucks behind opposition goaltenders during the 1981-82 season. When he realized that opposing teams were double-teaming him, he changed his style of play by becoming the NHL's premier set-up artist. In fact, in three of the nine seasons Gretzky led the NHL in scoring, he had more assists than the next leading scorer had points. Now there's a record that will never be duplicated!

While the Great One was a dominating force throughout the 1980s, he had to share the stage with two teammates who are also destined to be remembered as legends. Few players – in any era – can match Mark Messier's ability to provide leadership, timely scoring and bone-crunching body checks. He and his old teammate Wayne Gretzky are the only players to win the Hart Trophy with two different teams, but Messier is the only player in NHL history to captain two different teams (the Oilers and the Rangers) to a Stanley Cup title.

When Paul Coffey first arrived in Edmonton, many fans felt he would be too frail to be an effective defenseman in the rough and tumble NHL. But Coffey proved that in order to hit someone, you have to catch him first, and very few players can match the superior skating speed of Coffey. He has broken virtually every

Left: In his four full NHL seasons, Martin Brodeur registered 22 shutouts, the highest total for any NHL goaltender since Ken Dryden racked up 26 from 1971-72 to 1975-76.

Below: One of the bright, new array of stars being produced by the United States hockey system, Keith Tkachuk notched his first NHL goal-scoring crown in 1996-97 to become the first U.S.-born player to lead the league in goals.

Opposite left: The first freshman to win the Hobey Baker Trophy as the top U.S. college player, Paul Kariya also led Canada to its first World Hockey Championship title in 33 years by compiling 12 points in eight games as Canada captured the gold medal in 1994.

Opposite right: The first Vancouver Canuck player to win a major NHL award, Calder Trophy winner Pavel Bure also became the first Vancouver player to reach the 50-goal mark when he snapped 60 pucks past enemy goaltenders during the 1992-93 season.

all-time offensive record for defensemen, none more impressive than his 1985-86 performance of 48 goals and 138 points.

On the other side of the blueline, Patrick Roy has been the modern game's most influential goaltender, challenging even the legendary Jacques Plante. Many of today's netminders have modeled their style on Roy's, but none can match the master when the Stanley Cup is on the line. Martin Brodeur, who in 1997-98 is entering only his fifth full season in the league, has become so consistently excellent that his achievements are sometimes overlooked. Yet no goalie in the last 25 years can match the unbelievable numbers he chalked up in 1996-97.

Of the other NHL veterans still playing, few can equal the contributions of Ron Francis, Chris Chelios and Raymond Bourque. All three are over 35, but there's not a team in the league that wouldn't open up the bank vault if their services were for sale. Luckily for fans in Pittsburgh, Chicago and Boston, each member of this terrific trio will probably finish his career with his current team.

The league lost one of its all-time greatest talents

when Mario Lemieux – who averaged .832 goals per game during his career, a mark that may never be matched – decided to retire at the height of his ability in 1997. From the moment he stepped onto the ice – he scored his first NHL goal in his first shift, on his first shot in his first game – it was apparent that Lemieux was one of the those rare talents who could combine artistic grace with raw power and strength. While he was a reticent superstar who avoided the spotlight, he kept the Pittsburgh franchise on the NHL map, and brought the city its only two sports championships of the past 17 years.

Luckily for its millions of fans worldwide, the NHL features an exciting and alluring crop of young talent just waiting to assume the throne of greatness from Gretzky and Lemieux. From the board-crunching exploits of stay-at-home defender Ed Jovanovski to the acrobatic goaltending antics of Dominik Hasek to the quiet grace of playmaker and pace-setter Joe Sakic, the game appears ready to enter the new millennium. Eric Lindros, who at a hulking 6'4" and 240 pounds combines strength and resolute toughness with deft quickness, is the prototype for today's power forward. A speed demon such as Pavel Bure has the ability to lift fans out of seats every time the puck touches his stick. Vancouver fans were so eager to get a glimpse of their new superstar when he arrived from Russia that they filled the rink just to see his first practice with the club. The stick-handling wizardry of Jaromir Jagr combined with his breath-taking speed and Hollywood-chiseled profile make every on-ice move he makes instant highlight reel material. Add the likes of up-and-coming stars such as Paul Kariya, Keith Tkachuk and Martin Brodeur to the mix, and it appears that the game will continue to be on the upswing for years to come.

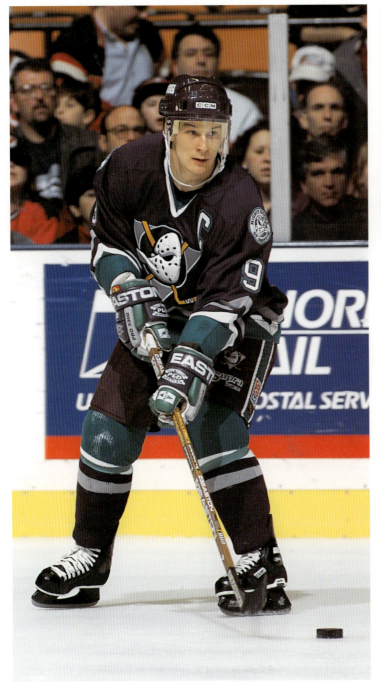

Jason Arnott

By using both his strength and clever offensive skills, Jason Arnott has quickly evolved into one of the NHL's top young talents. What Arnott brings to the mix cannot be measured in statistics, although he connected for 33 goals as a rookie and earned a berth on the NHL's All-Rookie Team; his main contribution is an intangible combination of leadership, motivation and gritty inspiration. Like Gary Roberts and Cam Neely before him, Arnott has the instincts to become the league's premier power forward.

He has one key trait that cannot be taught – hockey sense, which is the ability to make an instinctively correct decision about where to go or what to do during a play. He is an accurate shooter, an intelligent passer and a very fine skater. Former teammate Shayne Corson said, "It's fun to play with someone who is that skilled. He has the whole package."

Arnott uses his size and strength to deliver body-checks and get involved in physical battles on the ice. However, he is short-tempered, and his belligerency makes him prone to taking needless penalties. Arnott's drive probably will land him a captaincy within several years, and he's already one of the leaders on a young Oilers team.

Left: The Edmonton Oilers' first selection in the 1993 Entry Draft, Jason Arnott earned a berth on the NHL's All-Rookie Team after collecting 31 goals in his freshman campaign.

Jason Arnott

Position: **Center**
Height: **6'3"**
Weight: **220 lbs.**
Birth Date:
October 11, 1974
Birth Place:
Collingwood, Ontario
Drafted: **1993,**
Edmonton Oilers

Peter Bondra

Few players score more often than Peter Bondra, and few celebrate a goal as joyously as he does. Bondra simply loves to score – and on a defensive-minded Washington team, that's especially important.

After four promising but inconsistent seasons, Bondra joined the NHL's elite in 1994-95 by topping all NHL sharpshooters with 34 goals in 47 games during the NHL's lockout-shortened season. Capitals coach Jim Schoenfeld said an off-season conditioning program was the main reason for Bondra's leap forward. "He became a more complete player," said Schoenfeld. "He got more ice time because he was stronger and more aggressive." With his new-found strength, Bondra could power through checkers and create more scoring chances.

Bondra's exceptional skating is another key to his success. Teammate Michal Pivonka said, "I've seen some fast guys, but when he gets going he's one of the fastest. The first couple of years he had the speed, but he didn't know how to use it. Now he's learning how to drive to the net or go wide."

A natural goal-scorer, Bondra can connect with a backhand, slapshot or a wrist shot, all of them released quickly and accurately. Bondra excels at killing penalties and scores more than his share of shorthanded goals. He does not create plays nearly as well as he finishes them – he is the only player in NHL history to lead the league in goals and not finish among the top 25 scorers – but as long as he keeps the red light glowing, the Capitals will be soaring.

Left: One of the NHL's top sharpshooters, Peter Bondra led the Washington Capitals in goals (46), power-play goals (10), shorthanded goals (4) and shots (314) during the 1996-97 season.

Peter Bondra

Position: **Right Wing**
Height: **6'1"**
Weight: **200 lbs.**
Birth Date:
February 7, 1968
Birth Place:
Luck, USSR
Drafted: **1990,**
Washington Capitals

Ray Bourque

No-one who has ever strapped on the blades has played defense as consistently as Boston's Ray Bourque, and it's doubtful that anyone ever will. Simple numbers tell the story – Bourque was selected to the NHL's First or Second All-Star Team in each of his first 17 seasons in the league. No other player, in any other professional sport, can match that streak of honor from the start of a career. In five of those campaigns, he also captured the Norris Trophy as the NHL's top rearguard.

Given the talent that has surrounded him during his 18 seasons with Boston, Bourque's accomplishments seem even more amazing. While the Bruins often appear to be contenders, they usually rely on hard work, not talent, to win games. Since Bourque has never had players of comparable ability around him, he has had to carry the team at both ends of the ice. And he does so impeccably. Boston general manager Harry Sinden declared, "When the other team has the puck in our end, he's the best defenseman who ever played." Colorado's Sandis Ozolinsh added, "He's the best there is now in terms of doing everything on the ice."

By using superb conditioning and natural strength to endure his heavy workload, Bourque has been able to avoid serious injury, even though opponents constantly target him with rough play. He plays physically himself, handing out crunching checks or tying up forwards in front of his net. He reads opposing

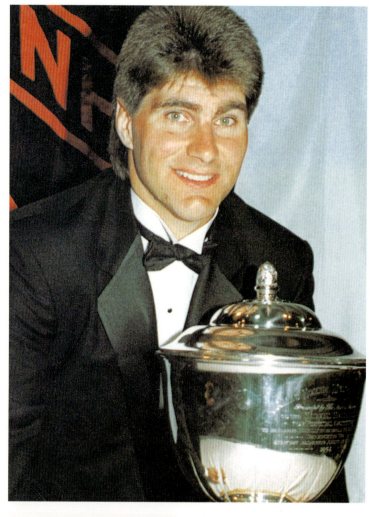

Above: Despite missing 20 games because of injuries during the 1996-97 schedule, Ray Bourque still finished third among defensemen with 19 goals. He is seen here with his third Norris Trophy in 1990.

Left: Bourque, who won the Calder Trophy in 1979-80, is the last member of the Boston Bruins to be selected as the NHL's top freshman.

Opposite: In 1992, Bourque received the King Clancy Trophy for his leadership qualities on and off the ice.

Ray Bourque

Position: **Defense**
Height: **5'11"**
Weight: **215 lbs.**
Birth Date:
December 28, 1960
Birth Place:
Montreal, Quebec
Drafted: **1979,
Boston Bruins**

attacks so well that he rarely makes an error or gets caught out of position in his own zone.

Bourque's excellent skating ability lets him start an attack. His puckhandling and passing skills equal that of most forwards, which means he can either carry the puck into the enemy zone or make a smart pass to a forward. His shot is so good that he has won the shooting accuracy competition at the NHL All-Star Game. Year after year, Bourque has ranked among the league leaders in shots on goal. In short, the Boston offense begins and often ends with him.

Although Bourque's 1996-97 campaign was slowed by injury, he became Boston's all-time leading scorer when he recorded his 1340th point. Afterwards, teammate Don Sweeney commented, "Very few players can make an impact on a franchise, and on a whole sport, over such a long period of time. He's in a very, very privileged group." Despite missing the playoffs for the first time since 1967, Boston fans do have something to cheer about: Bourque signed a contract extension that will be sure to keep him in a Bruins jersey for the remainder of his career.

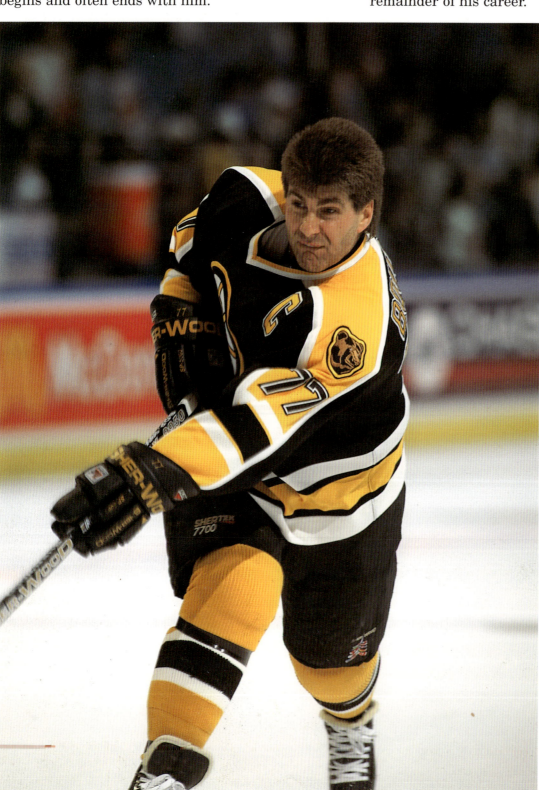

Left: Although he was hobbled by injury throughout much of the 1996-97 season, Bourque still led the Bruins in power-play goals (8) and game-winning goals (3).

Opposite above: Bourque's steady presence along the blueline helped Team Canada capture the Canada Cup championship in 1984 and 1991.

Opposite below: When Harry Sinden, veteran general manager of the Bruins, was asked when he planned to retire, Sinden answered, "Five minutes after Ray Bourque does."

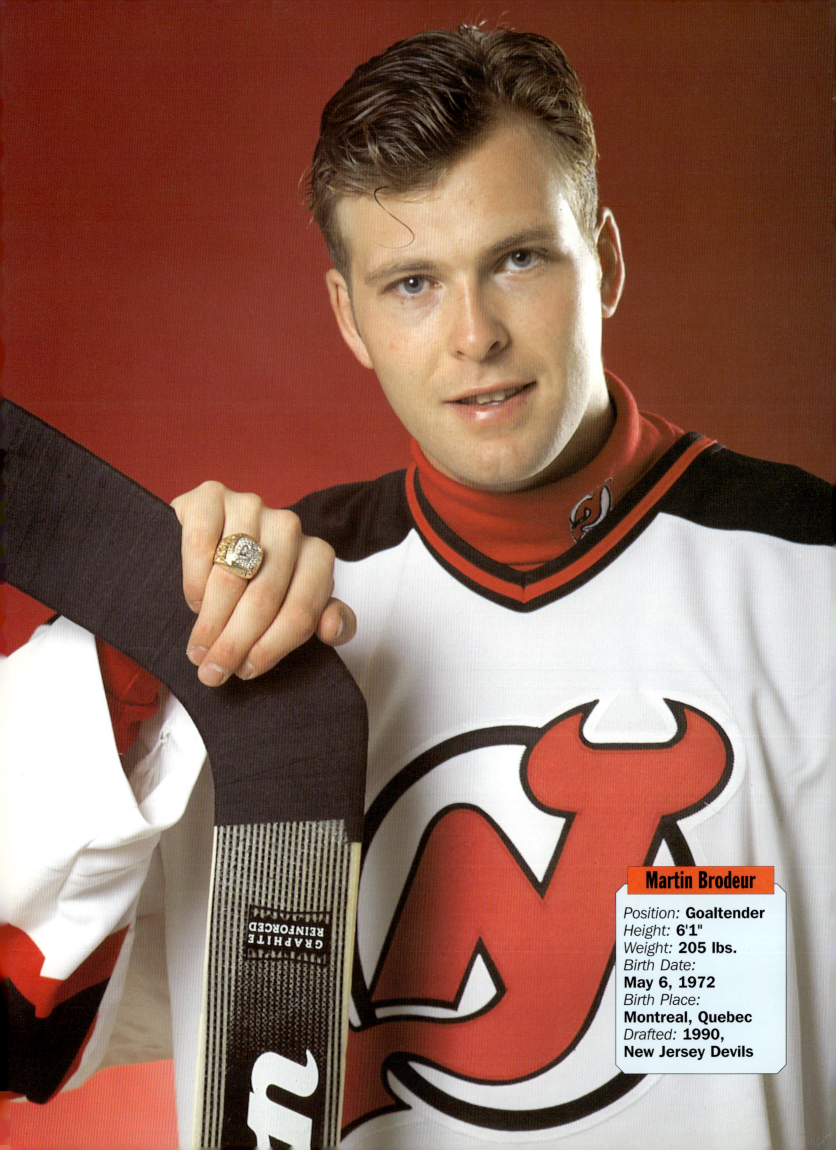

Martin Brodeur

Position: **Goaltender**
Height: **6'1"**
Weight: **205 lbs.**
Birth Date:
May 6, 1972
Birth Place:
Montreal, Quebec
Drafted: **1990,
New Jersey Devils**

Martin Brodeur

Like many French-Canadian goaltenders, Martin Brodeur grew up idolizing Patrick Roy, and like him, he has made an dramatic impact in the NHL. Brodeur has already captured the Calder Trophy as the NHL's best rookie, led the Devils to the Stanley Cup title in 1994-95 and played in a pair of NHL All-Star games.

Brodeur plays with remarkable poise and confidence, and he rarely looks unsettled in big games. In his first taste of post-season action, he recorded a 1.95 goals-against average as New Jersey reached the semi-finals. During the Devils' championship run in 1994-95, his average dipped to a remarkable 1.67. "Marty's confidence level seems to go up in the playoffs," said Jersey forward John MacLean. "He seems to rise to the challenge." Former NHL goalie Tim Bernhardt added, "He has always been able to make the big save when he has to."

Technically, Brodeur is very sound. Unlike most of today's young goalies, he plays a stand-up style, holding his large frame square to the shooter, which minimizes his mediocre skating ability. Only when necessary will he fall to the ice and use the butterfly

Opposite: Martin Brodeur's father, Denis, was an outstanding goaltender who served as the practice netminder for the Montreal Canadiens during the team's glory days in the 1950's.

Above: One of Brodeur's great assets is his elasticity, which enables him to regain his feet quickly after making a tough save and allows him to stretch and cover all the corners of the net.

Right: After making his NHL debut during the 1991-92 campaign, Brodeur spent the entire 1992-93 season in the minors with the American Hockey League's Utica Devils.

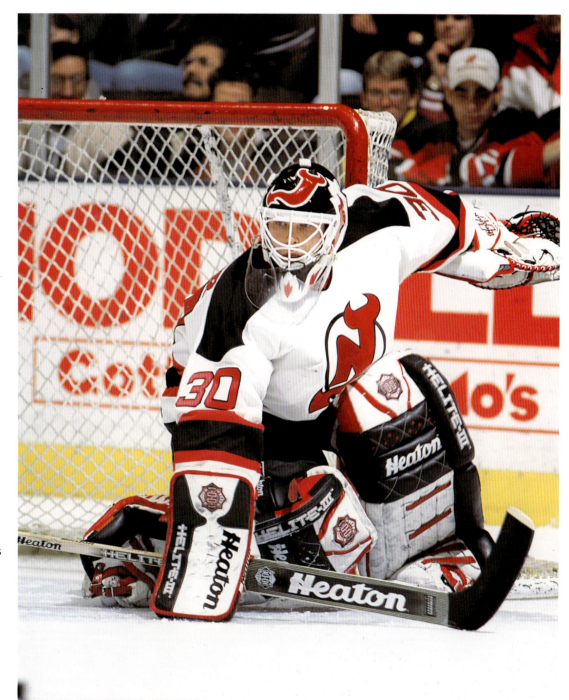

Opposite: Although Brodeur struggled in his first pro season in the minors, he still won the goaltender's job with the Devils in 1993-94. He went on to win the Calder Trophy as the league's top freshman, recording a GAA of 2.40.

Right: In 1994-95, only his second full NHL campaign, Brodeur helped lead the Devils to the franchise's first Stanley Cup title, leading all playoff goalies in games (20), wins (16), shutouts (3) and GAA (1.67).

Below: In 1996-97, Martin Brodeur established New Jersey franchise records for wins (37), shutouts (10) and goals-against average (1.88).

technique. New Jersey coach Jacques Lemaire praised his "great glove" and said "his movement is quick for a big guy." Lemaire added that Brodeur has an inborn ability to read plays as they develop in front of him.

While it's true that Brodeur benefits from his team's suffocating defensive style, he proved he could win games without much offensive help in 1995-96. The Devils averaged only 2.6 goals a game and missed the playoffs, yet Brodeur managed 34 wins. In 1996-97, he had the finest season of any goaltender in the quarter-century, posting a league-leading ten shutouts on his way to a league-leading goals-against average of 1.88. That season, Brodeur became the first netminder since Ken Dryden to reach double figures in shutouts, and his GAA was the lowest since Tony Esposito's mark of 1.77 in 1971-72.

Pavel Bure

His nickname – The Russian Rocket – describes his style perfectly: fast, powerful, even exhilarating. Pavel Bure is one of the most exciting players to play in the NHL in some time.

In 1995-96 and 1996-97, Bure was hit with serious injuries, but when he's healthy, his game radiates a raw energy that causes a constant buzz among the crowd. Though small, he has tremendously strong thigh muscles, and these propel him down the ice at great speed. Bure executes quick, dazzling moves on the rush, the kind that make observers gasp with wonder. He has a powerful shot that he unleashes frequently. "He's a tremendous talent," said Vancouver general manager Pat Quinn. "He has the speed and he has such great instincts on the ice."

Bure is an intense player who owns a bit of a mean streak. He can play a physical, chippy style, the kind that's more often seen from a grinder than a goal-scorer. A true athlete who is committed to the game and keeps himself in top shape, Bure derives his natural talent and work ethic from his father, an Olympic champion swimmer.

Few players are more valuable to their team than Bure. Before he arrived in Vancouver, the team had endured 15 consecutive losing seasons. Once he joined the Canucks in 1991-92, they promptly became a Stanley Cup contender. In 1993-94, he led the Canucks to the Stanley Cup finals with an inspired performance, recording 31 points in 24 games. The future success of the Canucks rides mainly on his shoulders.

Left: While injuries derailed the Russian Rocket in 1995-96 and 1996-97, Pavel Bure remains one of the most talented players in the NHL. It took Bure only 154 games to score his first 100 NHL goals, making him only the sixth player in NHL history to reach the century mark in goals in less than 155 games.

Opposite: Pavel Bure learned to refine many of his skills from his father, who was a member of the Soviet swimming team and competed in the 1968, 1972 and 1976 Olympic Games.

Pavel Bure

Position: **Right Wing**
Height: **5'10"**
Weight: **189 lbs.**
Birth Date:
March 31, 1971
Birth Place:
Moscow, USSR
Drafted: **1989,
Vancouver Canucks**

Chris Chelios

In one of the most lopsided trades in history, the Montreal Canadiens sent Chris Chelios, only one year removed from winning the Norris Trophy as the league's top rearguard, to Chicago for an aging Denis Savard. The fiery, intense defenseman has been the heart of the Blackhawks ever since.

Chelios is a special player, the kind who is deeply respected by opponents and loved by teammates. Former Blackhawk Bernie Nicholls said, "If I had to choose to play my whole career with one guy, it would be Chris. He's the best teammate I've ever had." Chelios inspires such feelings with his honesty, loyalty, toughness – and hard work. Teammate Steve Smith noted, "Of all the stars I've played with, Chris is by far the most dedicated athlete."

The Chicago organization recognizes his value. In December 1996, after signing Chelios to a three-year contract, Chicago general manager Bob Pulford stated: "He certainly is one of the great players in hockey, probably a Hall of Famer and he should end his career in Chicago."

Along with Ray Bourque, Chelios is considered the most complete blueliner in the NHL. Since he plays for

Above: Chris Chelios added a third Norris Trophy to his collection in 1996.

Left: Chelios is at his best when around the Hawks' crease, clearing opposing forwards from in front of the Chicago goal.

Opposite: Chelios was named as the Blackhawks captain prior to the 1995-96 season.

Chris Chelios

Position: **Defense**
Height: **6'1"**
Weight: **186 lbs.**
Birth Date:
January 25, 1962
Birth Place:
Chicago, Illinois
Drafted: **1981,**
Montreal Canadiens

a defensive-styled team, his scoring totals are lower than they might be, but he still records good numbers. Chelios is a power-play specialist who can set up forwards with alert passes or score off a hard slapshot. In five-on-five situations, he is often called on to be the one to start a rush.

Defensively, the three-time Norris Trophy winner can do anything that's required. He's not large by NHL standards, but he plays like a big man, handing out checks and wrestling fearlessly with opponents. He moves the puck quickly out of his own zone, and he is an outstanding penalty killer. His fluid skating helps him in every defensive situation.

Chelios is so combative that he can be pushed into taking bad penalties. In recent seasons, he has learned to control his temper, but he'll never be a candidate for the Lady Byng Trophy. In many ways, he is a throwback to the six-team era, a defenseman who stands his ground and plays the game on his terms. If you come into his kitchen, you'd better be able to stand the heat.

Despite the fact that he is 35 years old and has recorded an enormous amount of ice time over the years, he never seems to slow down. Former teammate Jeremy Roenick said, "Chelly gets better with age. It doesn't mean anything to him." That's the best news of all for Chicago fans.

Paul Coffey

If Bobby Orr was the most offensively creative defenseman in history, Paul Coffey ranks a close second. Coffey's unparalleled skating ability and abundant talent have allowed him to become the NHL's all-time leading scorer among defensemen in goals, assists and points.

Coffey spent his first seven seasons with the Edmonton Oilers, a team that fitted his talent perfectly. The Oilers introduced a European style of play to the NHL, using speed and shiftiness to mount constant, dizzying attacks. Coffey often started these assaults, gliding down the ice with the puck, sliding or accelerating past would-be checkers with ease. On a team of fabulous skaters, he was the best.

It is Coffey's great passing skill that enabled him to reach the 1,000 career assist mark in 1995-96. He is the first defenseman and the fourth player in history to hit this plateau. His trademark is the home-run

Opposite: Chelios, who spent seven seasons with the Habs before being traded to the Blackhawks, became the first defenseman to lead Chicago in scoring during the 1995-96 season, collecting 14 goals and 58 assists. Those totals earned the Chicago native a berth on the NHL's All-Star First Team and earned him his second Norris Trophy as a member of the Hawks.

Right: One of the most gifted offensive rearguards in NHL history, Paul Coffey has reached the 100-point plateau five times during his 17 seasons in the league.

Paul Coffey

Position: **Defense**
Height: **6'0"**
Weight: **190 lbs.**
Birth Date:
June 1, 1961
Birth Place:
Weston, Ontario
Drafted: **1980,
Edmonton Oilers**

Left: Coffey was traded to the Philadelphia Flyers by the Hartford Whalers on December 15, 1996.

Below: After winning three championships with the Edmonton Oilers, Coffey returned to the Stanley Cup winner's circle in 1991-92 with the Pittsburgh Penguins.

pass, a long, breakaway feed that is delivered right to the blade of a forward. This kind of play requires awareness and vision, two traits Coffey owns in abundance. "I don't think I've ever played with anybody who sees the ice as well," said former teammate Ray Sheppard. He is also a quick thinker, and Philadelphia general manager Bob Clarke said, "He needs people who can think as fast as he does."

Now a member of the Philadelphia Flyers, Coffey is primarily a playmaker, but he was a deadly goal-scorer in his prime Edmonton years. He had two 40-goal seasons, and he holds the single-season record for defensemen with 48 – a mark that may never fall. He

That rare combination of offensive and defensive ability has put a heavy load on Fedorov's shoulders. Not only is he expected to contribute offensively, on many evenings he is also expected to shut down the opposition's number one center. So while it's true his point totals have waned somewhat over the past two seasons, his dedication to defense has not. He won his second Selke Trophy in 1995-96 and finished among the league leaders in plus/minus with a plus 29 in 1996-97.

And his teammates have not lost faith in their great defender. "Sergei is a game-breaker for us any time he's on the ice," said Detroit captain Steve Yzerman. "He's the most talented player I've ever seen, and I don't think there's any reason why he shouldn't dominate every night."

Theoren Fleury

In an era when the ideal forward is supposed to be over six feet tall and weigh 200 pounds, Theoren Fleury reminds us that you cannot measure heart and desire in inches and pounds. Fleury may be the NHL's smallest skater, but he's also the Calgary Flames' most valuable player.

Fleury is a hard worker who annoys opponents with his determined, chippy play. He once described himself as the Flames' "spark, the pick-me-up, the one to light the fuse." This type of player is not usually a big point producer, but Fleury is an exception. A quick, agile skater, he can slip around or through defenders, and he's fast enough to outrace almost all of them. He finishes plays well with his fine wrist shot.

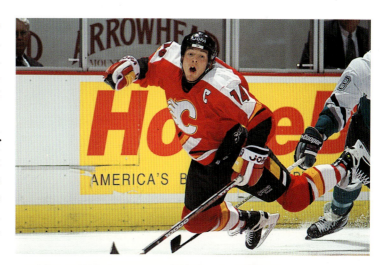

Opposite: Fedorov remains dedicated to defense, finishing the 1996-97 season with a plus/minus rating of +29.

Above right: The Calgary Flames acknowledged Theoren Fleury's value to the team by appointing him the team captain in 1995.

Right: Fleury's ability to maneuver through traffic has been one of his greatest traits.

Theoren Fleury	
Position:	**Right Wing/Center**
Height:	**5'6"**
Weight:	**160 lbs.**
Birth Date:	**June 29, 1968**
Birth Place:	**Oxbow, Saskatchewan**
Drafted:	**1987, Calgary Flames**

Left: Renowned as the spark that fuels the Flames, Fleury led Calgary in goals (29), assists (38), points (67), and shots-on-goal (336) during the 1996-97 season.

With his ability to weave through traffic and skate in any situation, Fleury has become a mainstay on the power play and penalty kill, and even when playing wing, he will take quite a few faceoffs. He doesn't hesitate to backcheck or get entangled with much bigger opponents. His former coach Terry Crisp commented, "Besides being very talented, this kid is a pistol and he fears nobody."

In 1995-96, Fleury had to deal with an adversary of a different kind: Crohn's Disease, an intestinal ailment. He struggled in the first month of the season but finished strongly with 96 points, an amazing total under the circumstances. Although he still has recurring bouts with the disease he was able to lead the Flames in scoring for the fifth time in his nine seasons with the club in 1996-97.

Peter Forsberg

Before coming to North America in 1994, Peter Forsberg was considered the best player outside the NHL. Now, some would argue he's the best player in it.

Forsberg's four seasons in the Swedish Elite League allowed him to jump to the NHL with a fully-formed game. He has the offensive ability that you expect from a European skater, yet he has the physical game of a top checking forward. Forsberg represents the ideal blend of Eastern and Western hockey. "He has the whole package," enthused teammate Mike Ricci. "He's big, strong, skates well and he hits hard. He's way more physical than a lot of skilled players."

With his strength, balance and great skating ability, Forsberg makes it very difficult for opponents to

Left: One of the most talented all-around performers in the game, Peter Forsberg was acquired by the Quebec Nordiques (now the Colorado Avalanche) in the Eric Lindros trade in June 1992. The hard-hitting, sweet-skating Swede led the Avalanche in scoring in 1996-97 with 86 points in only 65 games.

Peter Forsberg
Position: **Center**
Height: **6'0"**
Weight: **190 lbs.**
Birth Date: **July 20, 1973**
Birth Place: **Ornskoldsvik, Sweden**
Drafted: **1991, Philadelphia Flyers**

Ron Francis

During his 16 seasons, Ron Francis has been one of the most consistent and efficient players in the league – but for a long time, not many people noticed him.

Francis spent the first decade of his career in Hartford, toiling for a mediocre club in a small market location that had little playoff success. Francis isn't eye-catching – he succeeds by doing everything well, and he plays a "quiet" game on the ice, without the dazzling stickhandling, arm-pumping enthusiasm of some of today's younger stars.

Nevertheless, Detroit assistant coach Barry Smith has called him an "extraordinary hockey player. He can win faceoffs in either zone, puts up great stats every year and is very smart in his defensive play. He reads the game so well, and he has excellent puck skills – he can put it by somebody, he can hold it and he can control it."

Francis finally gained widespread recognition after he was traded to Pittsburgh in his tenth season. He fit-

Opposite: With an Olympic gold medal (won with Sweden in 1994) and a Stanley Cup ring already to his credit, many experts predict that Peter Forsberg will be adding a scoring title and an MVP award to his trophy shelf soon.

Above right: Ron Francis reached another NHL milestone when he notched his 400th career goal during Pittsburgh's 4-1 victory over the Los Angeles Kings on March 29, 1997.

Right: Now entering his 17th NHL season, Ron Francis remains one of the league's top set-up artists; he has collected at least 50 assists 12 times.

Ron Francis

Position: **Center**
Height: **6'2"**
Weight: **200 lbs.**
Birth Date:
March 1, 1963
Birth Place: **Sault Ste. Marie, Ontario**
Drafted: **1981, Hartford Whalers**

Toronto, one of his first moves was to acquire Gilmour. In his first full season with the Leafs in 1992-93, Gilmour carried Toronto into the semi-finals for the first time since 1978 and duplicated the feat the following season. In those two seasons, Gilmour was the most complete two-way player in the game, a fact that was duly noted when he was awarded the Selke Trophy in 1993, becoming the first Leaf player to win a major NHL award in 26 years.

His play was consistently inspired – every time he stepped on the ice, he seemed to control the puck or make a timely defensive play. Fletcher himself noted that, "He's the type of guy you win Stanley Cups with." Unfortunately for Gilmour and the Leafs, the club couldn't maintain its upward course and Gilmour was traded to New Jersey late in the 1996-97 season for three young players, each of whom had similarities to the departing captain. In his brief five-season career in Toronto, Gilmour set a plethora of team records and became the club's all-time leader in post-season points.

After Gilmour was traded from Toronto to New Jersey in February 1997, Jersey general manager Lou Lamoriello stated, "Doug has what I call sheer ability. He makes the players around him so much better and he does it without sacrificing defense." Gilmour's game has been reborn in New Jersey, and the team went on to lose only 5 of its 22 games with him in the lineup.

Defensively, his agility, skating prowess and work ethic enable him to check anyone. Offensively, Gilmour creates scoring chances with quick, clever moves and allows his linemates to finish. His anticipation and passing skills are first-rate, which means his wingers usually are in the right place to score when they receive the puck. Like Gretzky, he excels at setting up teammates from behind the opposing net. Gilmour's most important attribute is his intense desire to win, which infects and excites his team.

Opposite: An often overlooked aspect of Gilmour's game is his ability to win key face-offs and control his opposing centermen after the draw.

Above: During the 1992-93 playoffs, Gilmour was an unstoppable force, leading all post-season scorers with 25 assists despite the fact that the Maple Leafs failed to advance to the final round.

Right: Gilmour ensured that his name would be forever etched in post-season lore by scoring the Stanley Cup-winning goal in the Calgary Flames' six-game victory over Montreal in the 1989 finals.

Wayne Gretzky

No-one ever has dominated a North American team sport like Wayne Gretzky. When he came into the NHL, many observers thought he was too small and frail to succeed, but Gretzky used his unmatched talent and great determination to scale previously unreachable heights.

While he wasn't the first center to play an all-out, attacking style – Marcel Dionne and Gilbert Perreault were two notables who preceded him – Gretzky is the one who perfected it. His remarkable skating is the foundation of his game: apart from being fast, Gretzky has near-perfect agility and balance. He is so elusive and has so many clever moves that checking him is a real challenge. He is also the greatest passer in the history of the sport. Quite simply, there is no pass he cannot complete. His hand skills are so strong that he can easily bat a puck out of the air and control it.

When he has the puck, it appears to be nailed to his stick. He owns a breathtaking backhand, an excellent wrist shot and an under-appreciated slapshot.

Another key to Gretzky's success is his anticipation – a quality his father taught him at an early age. He can look at the ice and, in an instant, recognize the patterns in front of him. If he doesn't have the puck, he knows where he should go to intercept or receive it. If he has it, he understands how and when to make the right pass, the one that will create a dangerous scoring chance. Because he's always thinking ahead, Gretzky is the rare athlete who seems to command time. He never hurries, and he's famous for forcing defenders or goalies into making the first move.

The man is such an incredible talent that even his opponents have to admire him. Defenseman Dave Babych once observed, "There are times when you sit

Left: While Mark Messier is still the captain of the NY Rangers, Wayne Gretzky wore the "C" when Messier was injured during the 1996-97 campaign.

Opposite: For the first time since the 1987-88 season, Wayne Gretzky and Mark Messier were reunited as NHL teammates when Gretzky was signed by the Broadway Blues as a free agent. The Great One shone on the Great White Way, leading the team in scoring with 97 points.

Wayne Gretzky

Position: **Center**
Height: **6'0"**
Weight: **180 lbs.**
Birth Date:
January 26, 1961
Birth Place:
Brantford, Ontario
Drafted: **1979,
Edmonton Oilers**

Left: Gretzky and Rangers teammate Brian Leetch struggle for position during the inaugural World Cup Tournament, held in September 1996.

Below: When the King joined the L.A. Kings, he made hockey the "in" sport on the Hollywood social calendar. It was during Gretzky's stay in L.A. that he became the all-time leading scorer in the history of the NHL.

Opposite: Many of Gretzky's greatest accomplishments came during his eight seasons with the Edmonton Oilers. In 1983, 1986 and 1987, he had more assists than the next-leading scorer had points, something that had never happened before and may never happen again.

on the bench and you almost want to clap your hands at some of the things he does. One day I'm going to shake his hand and hope that some of his magic rubs off on me."

A unique element of the Gretzky legend is the fact that he achieved so much at an early age. When he joined the now-defunct World Hockey Association in 1979-80, he not only won Rookie of the Year honors, he also signed a multi-million dollar 10-year personal services contract with Peter Pocklington and helped lead the Edmonton Oilers into the WHA finals, all at the age of 18. The following year, the NHL expanded to include four former WHA franchises, and Gretzky finally got his chance to shine in the NHL. Although the league power-mongers ruled that the soon-to-be-Great One could not be considered a rookie, Gretzky set numerous records for a first-year player. He tied for the scoring lead with 137 points, became the youngest player ever to reach the 50-goal plateau and won the Hart Trophy as league MVP, another eye-opening achievement. And to all those critics who dismissed him as being "too young, too fragile, too slow" to excel at the top level, Gretzky proved he was to be a permanent fixture in the NHL.

Gretzky owns or shares more than 60 individual records in the NHL Guide and Record Book, many of which may never be broken. He is the NHL's all-time leader in goals, assists and points in both regular season and post-season play. Entering the 1997-98 season, he had 862 goals, 1843 assists and 2705 points, each one a record. His assist and point records likely never will fall, although there are one or two current players who might challenge his goal mark. Add his 10 scoring titles and nine MVP awards to the list, and it's clear that Gretzky is indeed the "Great One."

Dominik Hasek

Dominik Hasek looks like an acrobat more than a goalie, but his ability to stop the puck proves that he's no circus performer. "The Dominator" is the most spectacular goalie in the NHL, and arguably the best. Over the past four seasons, Hasek has led the league in save percentage four times and won the Vezina Trophy twice as the league's top twine-tender. In 1993-94, he recorded a goals-against average of 1.95, the lowest GAA since Bernie Parent's 1.89 average in the 1973-74 season. Early in the 1996-97 season, the Sabres lost captain and on-ice leader Pat Lafontaine for the rest of the campaign when he suffered a serious head injury. Hasek stepped up, and carried Buffalo into the play-offs with one of the greatest exhibitions of goaltending in the modern era of the game. He won a career-high 37 games and gave his young Buffalo teammates the confidence they needed to just go out and play their game. If they made a mistake, Hasek was there to bail them out.

Critics can point to many technical flaws in Hasek's style, but he knows exactly what he's doing in the

Above: Despite his peculiar, contortionist-like style, Dominik Hasek has been the NHL's dominant goaltender since joining the Buffalo Sabres.

Left: Hasek stacks the pads to stone NY Ranger forward Darren Langdon.

Opposite: After accosting a Buffalo sportswriter during the opening round of the 1997 playoffs, Hasek became the first goaltender in league history to be suspended during the post-season for an off-ice incident.

Dominik Hasek

Position: **Goaltender**
Height: **5'11"**
Weight: **168 lbs.**
Birth Date:
January 29, 1965
Birth Place:
Pardubice, Czechoslovakia
Drafted: **1983, Chicago Blackhawks**

crease. He'll dive and flop wildly, drop his stick along the goal-line and grab the puck with his blocker or make a save while lying on his back. But his reflexes, particularly his feet, are so quick they make up for his unorthodox moves.

Blessed with almost elastic flexibility, Hasek can twist and contort himself on the ice to make the impos- sible seem easy. Philadelphia coach Terry Murray said, "His pads cover post-to-post better than anyone in hockey. It always appears there is no room to shoot."

Before coming to North America, Hasek enjoyed a long and successful career in Europe, but he doesn't appear to be close to retirement, and that's good news for Buffalo fans.

Phil Housley

When Phil Housley joined the Buffalo Sabres in 1982, Buffalo general manager Scotty Bowman said he was "the closest thing I've seen to Bobby Orr." Bowman didn't necessarily mean Housley would be as great as Orr, but it immediately placed unrealistic expectations on the young man's shoulders. Fifteen seasons later, as Housley closes in on 1,000 career points, it's clear he's managed to prosper in spite of this.

Housley was an early bloomer who became the first defenseman to enter the NHL directly from high school. Remarkably, he scored 19 goals and 66 points in his first year, then recorded 31 goals in 1983-84.

Opposite: Hasek, who made his NHL debut with Chicago, is seen here wearing one of the "original six" commemorative uniforms during the NHL's 75th Anniversary season in 1991-92.

Above right: Phil Housley and Detroit forward Kirk Maltby pursue a loose puck during the 1996-97 season, Housley's first with the Washington Capitals.

Right: Although he struggled to find his offensive touch early in the season, Housley still led all Capitals' rearguards in scoring during the 1996-97 schedule with 11 goals and 29 assists.

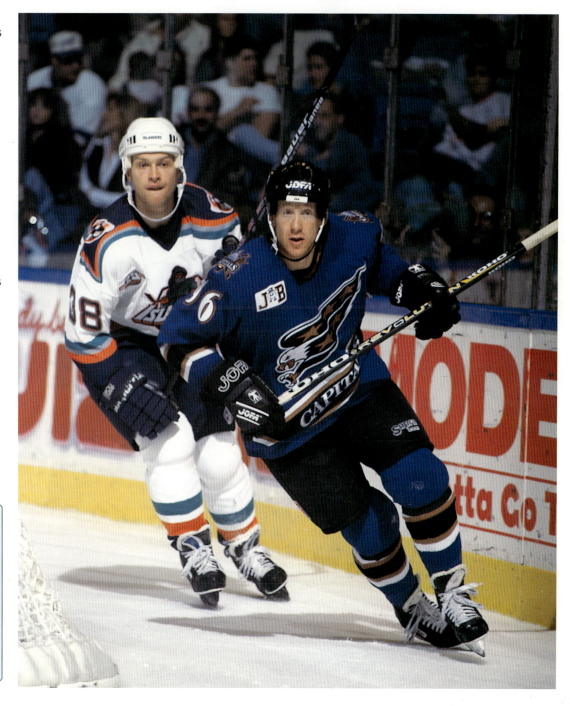

Phil Housley

Position: **Defense**
Height: **5'10"**
Weight: **185 lbs.**
Birth Date:
March 9, 1964
Birth Place:
St. Paul, Minnesota
Drafted: **1982,**
Buffalo Sabres

However, because of his size and pure scoring instincts, the team felt he might be a better forward. From his second season through his fourth, Housley played both positions.

When he plays within his limits, Housley can be very effective. Housley's vision is so acute that he can spot a developing attack by his team in a split-second and react quickly. If he chooses not to pass, he will use his speed and elusiveness to rush the puck. On the power play, his awareness and heavy shot make him invaluable.

In 1996-97, Housley joined Washington, his sixth team, and played his 1,000th game. "I still feel I have great jump and I think my mental grasp of the game can carry me another year or two," he said. The Washington Capitals and their fans hope that is true.

Opposite: Housley is the only American-born defenseman to score at least 20 goals in six consecutive seasons.

Above: One of only seven defensemen to score 30 goals in a single season, Housley needs only 10 points to become the fifth rearguard to reach the 1000-point plateau.

Right: Housley, seen here flattening the Philadelphia Flyers' Ron Sutter, is the only defenseman in hockey history to go directly from high school to the NHL.

Brett Hull

Brett Hull may have inherited some exceptional hockey genes, but his father can't take all the credit for his success. The son of Hall of Famer Bobby Hull, Brett has the same natural scoring ability as Dad, but the spark for his success did not come as naturally to Brett as it did to his dad.

When he was young, many observers felt Hull was an out-of-shape player with dubious skating ability. The Calgary Flames, who selected him in the sixth round of the 1984 Entry Draft, seemed to agree. In March 1986, Calgary traded the not-yet-golden Brett to St. Louis, even though he had scored 50 goals in the minors and recorded 50 points in 52 games with the Flames. No-one questioned his ability to shoot the puck, but everyone, including Hull himself, questioned his commitment. After a soul-searching summer, he decided to put all his energy into improving his game. In 1989-90, he answered his critics with an astonishing 72-goal performance and followed that up by setting an NHL record for right wingers with 86 goals in 1990-91. He won the Hart Trophy that year, making him and the Golden Jet the only father-son combo each to win the NHL's MVP award.

Hull is a consistently dangerous attacker because he has an uncanny ability to find open ice. Hull said he does this by "getting myself out of everyone's mind's eye." Once he slips through a hole, unnoticed, and receives a pass, Hull can unleash a heavy, fast shot in a split-second, without a backswing. No NHL player has a more lethal, accurate shot than Hull. In 1996-97, he scored his 500th goal in his 693rd game. Only three players have hit this mark in fewer games.

Left: Brett Hull, seen here unleashing the shot that has made him famous, is blessed with one of the quickest, most accurate shots of any right-winger ever to play the game.

Opposite: While he's never been known as a crafty stickhandler, Hull has developed into a highly effective passer, recording at least 40 assists in seven of his 10 full seasons in the league.

Brett Hull

Position: **Right Wing**
Height: **5'10"**
Weight: **201 lbs.**
Birth Date:
August 9, 1964
Birth Place:
Belleville, Ontario
Drafted: **1984,
Calgary Flames**

One part of Hull's game that is often overlooked is his excellent ability to set up his teammates with delicate, accurate passes. Blues assistant general manager Bob Berry said, "He is a great scorer first and always will be. But his ability to spot teammates in the open and get them the puck makes him more of a complete player."

Over the years, Hull has become more of a two-way winger. Although he went through a well-publicized feud with ex-coach Mike Keenan, Hull became more responsible defensively under Keenan's regime. He is a good penalty killer and he can also deliver a sound bodycheck.

Hull has attracted a lot of criticism and some praise for his outspoken ways. He is one of the few players in the league who always speaks his mind. In 1992, when St. Louis management traded his favorite center, Adam Oates, he was openly contemptuous of the move. Still, Hull is an on-ice leader who saves many of his best performances for big games. His supporting cast never has been good enough to win a Stanley Cup, but he proved he could lead a star-laden team to a championship. In September 1996, he helped guide Team USA to the 1996 World Cup Tournament title by leading the tournament in scoring with six goals and 10 points. Hull's ascension up the international scoring ladder may also be a curious trivia item in years to come. World Cup 1996 was the first international tournament in which Wayne Gretzky played but did not lead the tournament in total points.

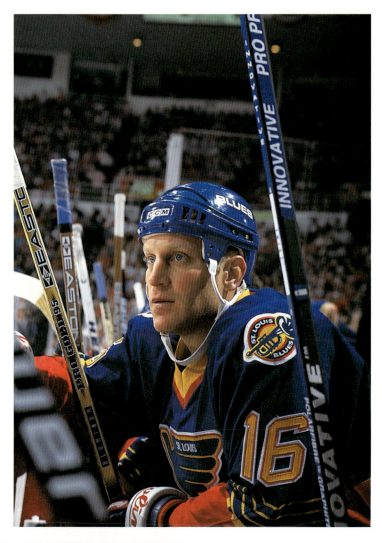

Above: After a much publicized dispute with coach/general manager Mike Keenan, Hull was stripped of his captaincy and relegated to the bench. When Keenan realized Hull couldn't score when he was sitting on the pine, he reinstated his star sniper but refused to give him back the captain's "C".

Left: In one of his finest on-ice performances, the Canadian-born Hull overcame the constant catcalls of the Canadian fans and led Team USA to the World Cup hockey championship in 1996.

Jaromir Jagr

One of the NHL's most unique, one-on-one talents, Jaromir Jagr draws as many off-ice accolades as on-ice defenders. Ranger coach Colin Campbell commented, "If he sets his mind to it, Jagr is virtually unstoppable. He is so big, so gifted and there isn't anything he won't do to score." Tampa Bay coach Terry Crisp wryly observes, "The best defense against him is to hope he's going to have an off-night."

A magician with the puck, Jagr is surprisingly creative for a player of his large size. He is so strong that he can score or set up a teammate while a defenseman (or two) is holding him. Most of the time, defenders can't even get near him. He is a fast and flawless skater who moves equally well laterally and forwards.

Once he has the puck, he controls it beautifully, and he can make any kind of deke at top speed. When the time comes to finish, Jagr often does so with a powerful, well-placed rocket. He is such a natural goal-scorer

Left: With the retirement of Mario Lemieux, Jaromir Jagr is the heir-apparent to reign as the game's dominant performer and the Penguins' offensive catalyst.

Jaromir Jagr

Position: **Right Wing**
Height: **6'2"**
Weight: **216 lbs.**
Birth Date:
February 15, 1972
Birth Place: **Kladno, Czechoslovakia**
Drafted: **1990, Pittsburgh Penguins**

that even Wayne Gretzky's single-season record of 92 goals may not be out of reach.

"Most of his goals are highlight-film goals," said New York Islanders scout Ken Morrow. "He has got power, finesse and skill. I think he's the best player in the league."

When Jagr first joined Pittsburgh, he played in Mario Lemieux's shadow. As Jagr matured and Lemieux missed long stretches with health problems, the Czech star took over the mantle of team leader and led both the team and the league in scoring with 32 goals and 38 assists in 1994-95. He followed that up with a 62-goal effort the following season, becoming just the 17th player to reach that plateau. Although a nagging groin injury caused him to miss 20 games during the 1996-97 campaign, he still managed to finish among the league leaders in goals (47) and points (95). Now that Mario Lemieux has retired, it's up to Jagr to lead the team back into the winner's circle.

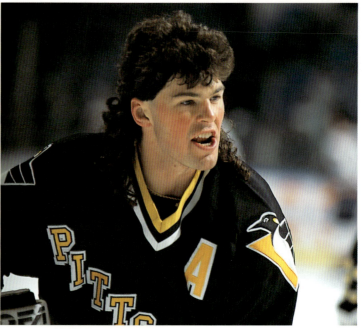

Above: With his stylishly long hair and magical moves on the ice, Jagr has become a heart-throb in Steel Town.

Left: When he's in full flight, there's no more electrifying presence on the ice than Jaromir Jagr. With his long reach, subtle moves and breathtaking speed, Jagr can dominate a game all by himself.

Opposite: Despite missing 19 games in 1996-97, Jagr still managed to finish sixth in league scoring with 47 goals and 95 points.

Ed Jovanovski

When Ed Jovanovski is on the ice, opponents have to keep their heads up and their eyes open. Though he's only played two seasons, the "Big Bopper" is one of the best open-ice hitters in the league and he has already set a high standard for tomorrow's group of young rearguards to follow.

As a number-one draft pick, Jovanovski was expected to make an immediate impact with the Florida Panthers in 1995-96. He did that and more, surprising some observers with his rapidly-maturing game. Florida management had been concerned that he might be caught out of position in his own zone, but with tutoring from assistant coach Lindy Ruff, he showed he could read plays well and react to them.

Jovanovski showed no fear either, playing aggressively and hitting with abandon. His physical play was an important part of Florida's march to the Cup final. The lasting image from Florida's quarterfinal win over Philadelphia is that of Jovanovski repeatedly belting Eric Lindros, the strongest player in the league. Not many rookies would attempt such a thing.

Jovanovski has the potential to become an offensive force as well. Florida president Bill Torrey noted, "He's a major-league puckhandler, he has an excellent shot and he's very offensive-minded." If Jovanovski can become a two-way defenseman like Ray Bourque or Chris Chelios, he should be the heart of the Panthers for the next decade.

Left: Ed Jovanovski finally got a grip on his potential during the 1995-96 season, becoming a dominant physical force along the Florida Panthers' blueline.

Ed Jovanovski

Position: **Defense**
Height: **6'2"**
Weight: **205 lbs.**
Birth Date:
June 26, 1976
Birth Place:
Windsor, Ontario
Drafted: **1994,**
Florida Panthers

Paul Kariya

During his brief university career with the University of Maine Black Bears, Paul Kariya was almost too good for the competition. He led the Black Bears to their only NCAA title and became the first freshman to win the Hobey Baker Trophy as the best college player in the country.

Now, after only three pro seasons, he appears ready to take his game to the next level and leave the rest of the NHL behind. After a terrific sophomore season that saw him reach both the 50-goal and 100-point plateaus, Kariya suffered a serious groin injury that forced him to miss the first 13 games of the 1996-97 campaign. Despite that setback, he still managed to collect 99 points and lead the Anaheim Mighty Ducks

Above left: Paul Kariya unleashes his patented "snap" shot that terrorized goaltenders throughout the 1996-97 season.

Left: One of the key elements of Kariya's game is his ability to see the whole ice surface and surmise within an instant where his teammates are going to be. It's a rare ability that only a few of the game's greats have been able to master.

Paul Kariya

Position: **Left Wing**
Height: **5'11"**
Weight: **175 lbs.**
Birth Date:
October 16, 1974
Birth Place: **Vancouver, British Columbia**
Drafted: **1993, Anaheim Mighty Ducks**

Left: Paul Kariya had another outstanding season for the Anaheim Mighty Ducks in 1996-97, leading the club in power-play goals (15), game-winning goals (10), and shots-on-goal (340). It's important to note that Kariya led the league in shots-on-goal despite missing 13 games during the season. Had he been healthy, he could have challenged the 400-shot plateau which has been reached by only two players in history: Phil Esposito and Bobby Hull.

into the playoffs for the first time in franchise history. "I think he's as close to being the next superstar in the game as there is," reflected Colorado coach Marc Crawford.

A player of Kariya's ability emerges once or twice every decade. He may not be the offensive equal of Pavel Bure, but his game is more complex; and while he cannot dominate physically like Eric Lindros, he has a better command of his defensive responsibilities. Every time he's on the ice, he seems to do something flashy. His puckhandling skills are so accomplished that they remind some observers of Wayne Gretzky's, and he loves to pass without looking. His shot is a laser that can be fired in the blink of an eye. "He has got everything you could possibly imagine in a hockey player," said Sergei Fedorov.

Kariya is very dedicated to the game, and he always looks for ways to improve. After his rookie season with Anaheim, he added ten pounds of muscle to his small frame, and it made a difference. "He makes good hard hits," said teammate Guy Hebert. "The word gets around the league. Players know he's not a frail kid." With the extra muscle and a renewed commitment to defense, Kariya is now a solid two-way player with the potential to become the heir apparent to the Gretzky-Lemieux throne.

John LeClair

John LeClair was a key part of the 1992-93 Stanley Cup champion Montreal Canadiens, yet he didn't become a star until he was traded to Philadelphia in 1994-95. The hard-shooting winger couldn't break out of his defensive role in Montreal, but playing next to Eric Lindros on the Legion of Doom Line has transformed him into one of the NHL's top snipers.

LeClair was always expected to be a big scorer, but in his three seasons in Montreal he was used mainly as a checker. He played center, a position he wasn't comfortable with, and he didn't shoot much. When he landed in Philadelphia, he immediately found his stride and won a surprising berth on the NHL's First All-Star Team. He climbed the 50-goal ladder for the first time in 1995-96 and made a return visit to the NHL's post-season All-Star squad. He continued his offensive onslaught in 1996-97, leading the Flyers in

Above: John LeClair celebrates a Team USA goal during the 1996 World Cup Tournament.

Left: John LeClair doing what he does best: searching for open ice to set up and fire his deadly accurate wrist shot at an unsuspecting goaltender.

John LeClair

Position: **Left Wing**
Height: **6'3"**
Weight: **226 lbs.**
Birth Date:
July 5, 1969
Birth Place: **St. Albans, Vermont**
Drafted: **1987, Montreal Canadiens**

goals (50), points (97) and shots-on-goal while proving himself to be the league's pre-eminent left-winger.

Perhaps the most valuable weapon in the LeClair arsenal is his overpowering shot. "Just ask the goalies," said former teammate Craig MacTavish. "They're constantly placing ice bags on their shoulders because of that 98-100 mile-an-hour fastball Johnny possesses." He is also an accurate shooter, and his sniping ability makes him a mainstay of the Flyers' power play. Like his linemates, LeClair skates well for a big man, and he's a good playmaker.

LeClair's hard-driving, board-crunching style is an invaluable asset to Philadelphia. With a talented supporting cast, he should excel for many years.

Brian Leetch

Brian Leetch doesn't like to talk about himself, but then again, he doesn't need to – his on-ice moves speak volumes about the man, his talent and his desire. Leetch owns a rare combination of speed, quickness and creativity that makes him one of the most breathtaking blueliners in the NHL.

Most importantly, Leetch is a true leader. In 1993-94, he led the New York Rangers to the Stanley Cup title, winning the Conn Smythe Trophy as playoff MVP. In 1996, he captained Team USA in the first World Cup tournament and excited fans with his fabulous ice-long rushes that keyed the American offense in their three-game, final-round victory over Team Canada.

Leetch is a complete offensive threat. He's a fast, agile skater who needs only a split-second to reach top speed. His passing skills are first-rate, and like his teammate, Wayne Gretzky, he is adept at receiving a

Opposite: LeClair, seen here antagonizing Toronto's Felix Potvin and Dave Ellett, became the first player since "Bones" Raleigh in 1950 to score two overtime goals in the championship series when he knocked a pair of O/T winners past L.A.'s Kelly Hrudey in the 1993 finals.

Right: While it's true Brian Leetch doesn't play an overly physical game, he can still mess it up along the boards with the best of them, as Montreal's Sebastien Bordeleau discovered during this New York-Montreal tilt.

Brian Leetch

Position: **Defense**
Height: **5'11"**
Weight: **190 lbs.**
Birth Date:
March 3, 1968
Birth Place: **Corpus Christi, Texas**
Drafted: **1986, New York Rangers**

Opposite: Leetch breaks free from a San Jose defender to orchestrate another Rangers' surge up the ice.

Right: Leetch led all NHL rearguards in assists (58) and points (78) during the 1996-97 season.

Below: One of the proudest moments of Leetch's career came prior to the 1996 World Cup Tournament, when he was named captain of Team USA.

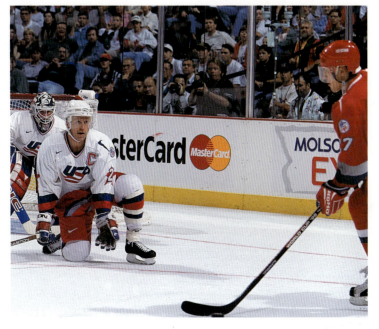

pass in mid-air. When he has the puck, he can execute a variety of clever, subtle moves or unleash a quick, accurate shot. During the 1996-97 campaign, he led all NHL blueliners in scoring with 78 points and reached the 20-goal mark for the fourth time in his career.

Despite his talent, Leetch is a humble star. After the Rangers captured the Cup in 1994, teammate Adam Graves boasted that "Leetch is the best defenseman since Bobby Orr." Leetch responded: "Everyone who has seen Bobby Orr knows that I am not a Bobby Orr. By far." Still, Leetch is in the prime of his career and, if he can avoid injury, should play well into the next decade.

Over the years, Leetch has matured into a reliable defender and penalty killer. He is not a very physical player, but he knows how to react in front of his net. Leetch uses his great lateral movement to cut off attackers and start the transition game.

Mario Lemieux

It will be a long, long time before hockey fans forget Mario Lemieux, who was arguably the greatest offensive talent in the history of the game. Lemieux not only played with more ease and grace than many of his predecessors, he had more offensive weapons and more ways to utilize them than any player in the league.

Unfortunately, Lemieux had a star-crossed career that resembled Bobby Orr's more than Wayne Gretzky's. Orr – probably the best defenseman ever –

played nine full seasons before retiring prematurely because his battered knees could not handle another operation. Lemieux, who battled back problems, cancer and anemia, announced that 1996-97 was his last season. Orr was 30 when he retired, Lemieux 31.

When he was able to play, Lemieux was simply dominating. Former Penguins coach Ed Johnston said, "I think he wants to leave the game being known as the best player ever," and many would say Lemieux

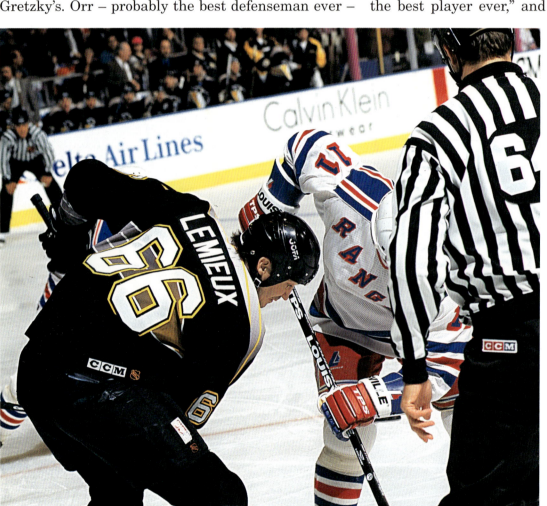

Left: Mario Lemieux, seen here winning a draw against NY Ranger captain Mark Messier, was a master in the face-off circle.

Opposite top: With his long reach and extraordinary strength, Lemieux was able to escape the clutches of opposing defenders. That power is evident here as he blocks off Florida blueliner Terry Carkner and smashes John Vanbiesbrouck's goalie stick in the process.

Opposite bottom: Lemieux became the seventh player in NHL history to record 600 career goals when he reached the magical milestone in Pittsburgh's 6-4 win over Vancouver on February 4, 1997.

Mario Lemieux

Position: **Center**
Height: **6'4"**
Weight: **225 lbs.**
Birth Date:
October 5, 1965
Birth Place:
Montreal, Quebec
Drafted: **1984, Pittsburgh Penguins**

achieved that. One reason behind his success was his unusual combination of hand skills and size. Wayne Gretzky remarked, "I've always told the guys, 'God, I wish I was his size.' I mean, the things he can do with the puck, the way he sees the game, it's so spectacular – I wish I had that reach." He added, "We hadn't seen a guy come into our sport who was 6'4" or 6'5" who had the kind of hands he had."

Lemieux's hands were magical. He owned every known stickhandling move and a few that never had been seen before. He had a soft, precise touch on his passes, yet his shot was stunningly quick and accurate. In his youth, he was a very fast, elusive skater. Illness and injury slowed Lemieux slightly in later years, but he still could dodge and feint defenders. In a game against the New Jersey Devils on December

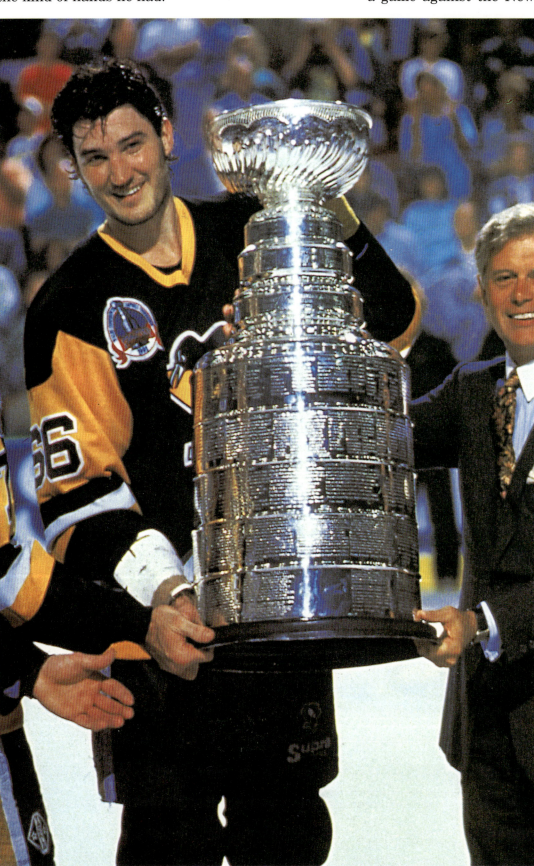

Left: Lemieux and Paul Coffey bask in the Stanley Cup spotlight following Pittsburgh's six-game victory over Minnesota in the 1992 championship finals.

Opposite top: Lemieux skirts the blueline in front of Chicago defender Chris Chelios during action in the 1993 Stanley Cup finals.

Opposite bottom: Lemieux joined Wayne Gretzky in leading Team Canada to the 1987 Canada Cup championship in an exciting three-game final against the Soviet National Team.

31, 1988, Lemieux became the first NHL player to score a goal in five different ways: shorthanded, on the power play, at regular strength, in the empty net and on a penalty shot.

Despite his natural talent, former Pittsburgh coach Scotty Bowman observed that Lemieux was also a calculating player. He didn't simply rely on his instincts, he also watched the play and decided what his best move should be. Because of this, Lemieux was almost unstoppable on breakaways. He scored goals with remarkable ease in every situation, and his career goals-per-game average is well over .800, the best in modern NHL history by far.

If he had been healthy, Lemieux may even have challenged most of Gretzky's records. As it was, his injury report sounds like a doctor's nightmare. He overcame bone infections and a herniated back only to be diagnosed with Hodgkin's Disease, a dangerous but highly curable form of cancer. Lemieux proved cancer could be beaten by returning to the NHL and in 1995-96 winning his fifth scoring title and his fourth Hart Trophy. Lemieux announced he would be retiring after the 1996-97 season, ensuring that he would close out his career as the first NHL player to retire after winning the scoring title.

Eric Lindros

Like Jean Beliveau, Bobby Orr, Guy Lafleur and Mario Lemieux before him, hockey fans began talking about Eric Lindros long before he actually arrived in the NHL. And like the Hall-of-Famers that preceded him, Lindros did not disappoint.

Lindros has an unparalleled combination of power and finesse in his game, traits that compare him favor-

ably with Mr. Hockey himself, Gordie Howe. No-one can match his upper body strength and few can equal his point-scoring ability. Despite his talent, Lindros often has received more attention for his off-ice activities. A strong-willed non-conformist, Lindros refused to play for Sault Ste. Marie in the Ontario junior league when the team drafted him. When the NHL's

Left: Eric Lindros is known as the "Total Package" in NHL circles because he has the size, strength and smarts to be the league's pre-eminent superstar.

Opposite: The only drawback to Lindros' aggressive style is that his constant banging and crashing has caused him to miss 103 games because of injury since joining the Flyers in 1992-93.

Eric Lindros

Position: **Center**
Height: **6'4"**
Weight: **236 lbs.**
Birth Date:
February 28, 1973
Birth Place:
London, Ontario
Drafted: **1991,
Quebec Nordiques**

Opposite: Despite missing 30 games because of a groin injury, Lindros still managed to compile 32 goals, 79 points and a team-leading seven game-winning goals during the 1996-97 season.

Right: Lindros, who in 1991 became the only non-professional to play for Team Canada in the Canada Cup series, also suited up for Canada during the 1996 World Cup Tournament.

Quebec Nordiques drafted him, he did the same. On both occasions, he got his way, but he lost some respect in the sporting community because of it.

Once in the NHL, Lindros became the heart of a previously lackluster Philadelphia team. He showed a passion for physical play, delivering thundering checks and battling for pucks along the boards. No opponent, not even Mark Messier, had the strength to subdue him. "People are physically afraid of him and they should be," said Flyers general manager Bob Clarke. "He's got that fire inside."

Lindros is a powerful skater who reaches top gear quickly. When he's charging down the ice, defensemen naturally back off. This allows him to drive to the net and deke the goalie or rifle a close-range snapshot. He is one of the most accurate shooters in the league, a skill that he's acquired through hard work. Whether he's giving or receiving passes, Lindros has a surprisingly soft touch. Philadelphia coach Terry Murray said Lindros has no patterns in his game, which makes him hard to defend against.

To some observers, Lindros is already the NHL's best. Florida coach Doug MacLean said, "Five-on-five, he is the most dominant player in the league. No doubt about it." Perhaps the only drawback to Lindros' immense abilities has been his inability to avoid injury. He suffered three knee injuries in his first four seasons and missed 18 games in the 1996-97 campaign but still managed to finish among the NHL's elite scorers with 31 goals and 79 points.

Al MacInnis

When Al MacInnis broke into the NHL, he was known primarily as a power play specialist, but now, fourteen seasons later, he has developed into one of the top rearguards of his era.

MacInnis is known far and wide for his cannon-like shot. "There's hard, then there is MacInnis hard," observed former goalie Mike Liut, but his five All-Star selections demonstrate that he has become a complete blueliner. The Calgary brass allowed MacInnis to develop at his own pace and the hulking rearguard spent the majority of his first three pro seasons in the minors before making it to the big leagues to stay. "He's a guy who's really had to work hard for any respect he's gotten," said former Calgary general manager Doug Risebrough. "When he broke into the league, he was a big shooter. That was all he could do. Then, when other parts of his game became a real plus – his skating, his defensive skills – people wouldn't look past his shot."

Unlike many of his contemporaries, MacInnis man-

Left: Al MacInnis, whose booming slapshot remains one of his greatest weapons, led all NHL blueliners with 296 shots-on-goal during the 1996-97 season.

Opposite: MacInnis, who has reached double figures in goals in 13 of his 14 full seasons in the league, notched a career-high 28 goals in 1992-93.

Al MacInnis

Position: **Defense**
Height: **6'2"**
Weight: **196 lbs.**
Birth Date:
July 11, 1963
Birth Place: **Inverness, Nova Scotia**
Drafted: **1981, Calgary Flames**

ages to play solid defense without being a hard hitter. He is fairly big, but he relies on positional play to neutralize opponents. His offensive skills are his main strength. MacInnis is a good puck-carrier who frequently joins the attack. When he sets up from the point in the opposing zone, he is very dangerous – he makes smart passes, and the threat of his shot makes defenders nervous.

In 1990-91, MacInnis had his finest season when he became only the fifth defenseman in league history to record 100 points in a season. However, in 1994-95, the Flames sent him to St. Louis, where Big Al has become the leader on the Blues' blueline. He'll long be remembered for his stellar play during the 1989 playoffs, when he won the Conn Smythe Trophy as the post-season MVP, and the Blues are confident that MacInnis can bring that level of play to St. Louis and help guide the Blues into the Stanley Cup winner's circle.

Mark Messier

"The first time I saw Messier play, I knew he was going to be a great player," said Glen Sather, Edmonton general manager. Sather is known as an astute judge of talent, but even he couldn't have foreseen just how dominant Messier would become. As he begins his 19th NHL season, Messier stands fifth on the all-time points list and ranks as one of the very best leaders in history, a remarkable achievement for a player who recorded only 33 points in his rookie season. He is one of only two players to win the Hart Trophy with two different teams, and is the only player to captain two different teams to the Stanley Cup championship. Despite an assortment of aches and pains, he still managed to reach the 35-goal and 80-point plateau in 1996-97.

Entering the 1997-98 season, Messier had nine major championships to his credit – six Stanley Cup titles and three Canada Cup crowns – more than anyone in the NHL except Edmonton blueliner Kevin Lowe. He consistently rises to the occasion in big games such as game six of the 1994 semi-finals, when the New York Rangers were facing elimination against

Opposite: Al MacInnis spent 13 seasons with the Calgary Flames before joining the St. Louis Blues prior to the 1994-95 season.

Right: A triumphant Mark Messier lifts Lord Stanley's Cup above his head to acknowledge the NY Rangers' first championship win since 1940, in 1993-94.

Mark Messier

Position: **Center**
Height: **6'1"**
Weight: **205 lbs.**
Birth Date:
January 18, 1961
Birth Place:
Edmonton, Alberta
Drafted: **1979,**
Edmonton Oilers

Opposite: Mark Messier has never been shy about driving to the net, as Florida defenders John Vanbiesbrouck (34) and Paul Laus found out during the Panthers' 5-2 win over the Broadway Blues on October 6, 1996.

Right: On May 4, 1997, Mark Messier set a new NHL record by appearing in his 228th career playoff game.

Below: Messier, who holds the NHL record for career shorthanded goals in the playoffs with 14, is one of the NHL's greatest two-way forwards.

New Jersey. Before the match, Messier guaranteed a Rangers victory, then backed it up with a hat trick in a 4-2 win. Afterwards, Jersey's John MacLean commented, "We had an opportunity to finish them off and he wouldn't let us. Only a special player could say what he did and then have the puck bounce for him the way it did."

Messier is the rare player who succeeds through sheer force of will and he is so competitive and intense that he forces his teammates to play at his level. By commanding as much respect from them as any coach, he is essentially a playing coach. Messier is not always a stern father figure, though. He has a warm, generous side, and he often invites new Rangers to stay with

him. In an era of individualism, Messier is the rare star who thinks and acts for his team first.

"Mess" plays a tough, complete game, hits and checks fearlessly and uses his powerful skating style to drive past or through his defenders. Messier has also created a patented offensive move that goalies still have not been able to solve. He drives down his off-wing and unleashes a ripping wrist shot off his back foot that invariably finds its way to the back of the net before the goaltender has an opportunity to react. Combine that with a deadly accurate backhand and a desire to go to the net and stay there, and you have the blueprint for the essential NHL weapon. And for the past 19 years, that has been Mark Messier.

Alexander Mogilny

Alexander Mogilny is the epitome of the enigmatic right-winger. On the upside, he's a devastating shooter who can out-race the breeze. On the other hand, he can be an unpredictable player, and that sometimes causes his game to fluctuate from brilliant to indifferent.

When he's on his game, Mogilny is two steps ahead of his opponents. Chicago's Gary Suter commented, "The thing that separates him from other guys is his anticipation. He has a knack for not coming too deep in his defensive zone, anticipating the turnover and

getting a step on the defenseman." Buffalo general manager John Muckler added, "You have to fear his speed but if you have body contact, he's so strong in the legs that he can break away from you."

One of the first Russian youngsters to play in the NHL, Mogilny showed slow but steady progress during his first three NHL seasons. Like many other Russian players, Mogilny needed time to adjust to North American culture, especially the constant air travel of the professional athlete. Although he was sometimes

Opposite: The smiles say it all as Messier, Steve Smith (left) and Jari Kurri celebrate the Oilers' first Cup win "A.G." (after Gretzky) on May 24, 1990.

Right: With his deft stickhandling and breakout speed, Alexander Mogilny has become one of the NHL's most exciting performers.

Alexander Mogilny

Position: **Right Wing**
Height: **5'11"**
Weight: **187 lbs.**
Birth Date:
February 18, 1969
Birth Place:
Khabarovsk, USSR
Drafted: **1988,**
Buffalo Sabres

Opposite: Mogilny celebrates one of his team-leading 31 goals during the 1996-97 campaign.

Right: Although he led the Vancouver Canucks in goals, assists and points during the 1996-97 season, Mogilny's totals and the team's performance suffered after teammate Pavel Bure was sidelined with a neck injury.

Below: When Buffalo Sabres captain Pat Lafontaine was injured during the 1992-93 season, Mogilny was handed the captain's reins for the rest of the campaign, becoming the first Russian-trained player to wear the "C".

moody, often lonely, he improved his goals, assists and points marks in each of his first three years with the Sabres. Then, in 1992-93, he suddenly exploded, connecting for a league-leading 76 goals and earning a berth on the NHL's Second All-Star Team. Although he never reached that level of success again, he continued to be a key offensive threat. In 1995, a dream came true for the right-wing Russian when he was traded to Vancouver, allowing him to play with his good friend and former junior teammate, Pavel Bure. Mogilny responded by reaching the 100-point mark for the second time in his career and earned another Second All-Star Team berth. The 1996-97 season was a difficult one for the Canucks and Mogilny, but he still managed to lead the team in six different offensive categories.

Sandis Ozolinsh

Sandis Ozolinsh showed he was ready for NHL stardom from the first moment he stepped on NHL ice. In 1992-93, his first full season in the league, he scored 26 goals, a truly remarkable feat for a sophomore defenseman.

A speedy skater, Ozolinsh won't hesitate to rush the puck. He is so eager to attack that he will try to intercept neutral zone passes and break into the opposing end. He often looks – and plays – more like a forward than a blueliner, a trait that has caused more than a few headaches for his coaches. But Colorado coach Marc Crawford put it all into perspective when he said, "He's probably one of our best chance producers. We certainly didn't get him to make him into a defensive defenseman."

Nevertheless, Ozolinsh showed signs in 1996-97 that he was becoming more conscious of his defensive duties. "The score of the game is important," he said. "If we're winning by one or two goals I'll only rush if I'm 100 percent sure I won't cost our team."

Ozolinsh was traded from a weak San Jose team to a powerful Colorado squad in October 1995, and it proved to be a good marriage. Colorado has plenty of talented forwards to take advantage of his break-out passes and his fine set-ups on the power play. Ozolinsh, who excelled in the 1995-96 playoffs, is just entering the prime years of his career, and if his 1996-97 numbers are any reflection – he led all defensemen in goals (23), power-play goals (13) and game-winning goals (4) – the best is yet to come.

Left: Sandis Ozolinsh makes up for the odd defensive lapse with his unique offensive talents, skills that allowed him to lead all NHL blueliners in goals (23) and power-play goals (13) during the 1996-97 season.

Sandis Ozolinsh

Position: **Defense**
Height: **6'1"**
Weight: **195 lbs.**
Birth Date:
August 3, 1972
Birth Place:
Riga, Latvia
Drafted: **1991,**
San Jose Sharks

Felix Potvin

As his nickname suggests, Felix "The Cat" Potvin is one of the quickest goalies in the NHL. He's also been one of the most consistent netminders in the league since he made his debut during the 1992-93 season.

One writer jokingly referred to Potvin as "Felix the Copycat" because his style is so similar to that of Patrick Roy, but that's not entirely true. Like Roy, Potvin is a butterfly goalie, but he doesn't challenge shooters as much as Roy does. He prefers to stand deep in his net with skates planted far apart. This is risky, because it limits his side-to-side movement and angle play, yet Potvin gets away with it. His butterfly style blocks the lower part of the net, where most shots are taken, and his great reflexes take care of most of the other shots.

Another of Potvin's great assets is his anticipation. Hartford forward Nelson Emerson praised Potvin by saying, "His strength is that he knows the game and the shooters. You shoot and you think it's going in, but he reacts so well to the play. He gets there in time."

Potvin's early maturation and relaxed attitude helped him succeed as soon as he joined the Leafs. He

Left: Felix Potvin, who led all NHL goalies with a 2.50 goals-against average in 1992-93, was the first Leaf goaltender to lead the NHL in GAA since Jacques Plante in 1970-71.

Felix Potvin

Position: **Goaltender**
Height: **6'0"**
Weight: **190 lbs.**
Birth Date:
June 23, 1971
Birth Place:
Anjou, Quebec
Drafted: **1990,
Toronto Maple Leafs**

was selected to the All-Rookie Team in 1992-93 and led the league with a 2.50 goals-against average – a truly outstanding feat for a first-year goalie. In Toronto's run to the semi-finals in 1993, Potvin played very well, leading all post-season goaltenders in games played (21) and minutes (1308). The following season, he backstopped the Leafs to the semi-finals again, recording three post-season shutouts along the way.

The 1996-97 season was a difficult one for both Potvin and his teammates. Toronto's team defense collapsed and as a result, Potvin struggled throughout the early part of the schedule, but made a fine recovery in the second half of the campaign. In the final 30 games of the season, Potvin once again displayed the form that made him one of the NHL's top crease cops and re-established his place among the goaltending elite. Certainly no goaltender faced as much rubber as Potvin did during the 1996-97 season. He led all goaltenders and set a Maple Leafs' team record by appearing in 74 games and also set an NHL record by facing a previously unheard of 2672 shots. Although he was rumored to be on the trade block during the season, general manager Cliff Fletcher turned down all requests for Potvin's services, and his play in the second half of the season proves he's still one of the NHL's top twine-tenders.

Mike Richter

Sitting in the quiet of the Team Canada dressing room after Team USA had just won the inaugural World Cup tournament, Canadian forward Theoren Fleury knew that one man more than anyone was responsible for his country's defeat. "I think Mike Richter should never have to buy another drink in his whole life," he said. "If ever there was a national hero it should be him. He was everything to them." To be sure, Richter put on a dazzling display in the deciding match of the World Cup. In the second period alone, he stopped 21 of 22 shots. Several times, Canada appeared to have a sure goal, but Richter's tremendous reflexes and quick lateral moves closed the door.

Richter's stature has grown considerably in the past five years. Always a good regular-season goalie, he drew a lot of criticism early in his career for allowing

Opposite top: Felix Potvin led all goaltenders in games played (21) and minutes (1308) during the 1992-93 playoffs.

Opposite bottom: While teammates like Matt Martin (3) seemed to be continually losing their balance, Potvin kept his despite facing an incredible 2672 shots during the 1996-97 season.

Right: Mike Richter won a career-high 42 games in helping lead the NY Rangers to a first-place finish during the 1993-94 season.

Mike Richter

Position: **Goaltender**
Height: **5'11"**
Weight: **185 lbs.**
Birth Date:
September 22, 1966
Birth Place: **Abington, Pennsylvania**
Drafted: **1985, New York Rangers**

bad goals at the worst of times. He turned the tables on his critics during the Rangers' run to the championship in 1993-94 by notching four shutouts and a 2.07 goals-against average.

While he receives a lot of praise for his athletic ability, Richter's former teammate Kevin Miller pointed out that "the key to his success is his tremendous work ethic. I've shot pucks at him a lot and I know how hard he works at his game. He's a real battler who hates being scored on in any circumstance, and it shows." Although there has been some concern in Ranger circles that Richter is growing "long in the tooth", he won 30 games in 1996-97 for only the second time in his career, proving to the brass and the fans there's still lots of life left in the "known Ranger".

Above: The Richter magic works its spell on Canada's Joe Sakic during the 1996 World Cup Tournament.

Left: Richter won 33 games for the NY Rangers during the 1996-97 schedule, the fourth highest total in the league.

Jeremy Roenick

Jeremy Roenick is an old-fashioned forward, the kind who throws himself at an enemy and the net with equal abandon. That reckless style causes havoc among opponents and has allowed Roenick to record a pair of 50-goal campaigns and rack up at least 100 points on three separate occasions. A pair of serious knee injuries have slowed his offensive production over the past two seasons, but that didn't prevent the Phoenix Coyotes from sending two players and a first round draft selection to Chicago to receive Roenick's services. When he joined Phoenix, coach Don Hay said, "We wanted his leadership, enthusiasm and passion for the game to rub off on the other players."

One of the most complete players in the game, Roenick's offensive skills are excellent, and if he chose to play a strict attacking style, he could rank among the very best scorers every year. He is fast enough to jet past defensemen, and he changes speed and direc-

Left: Jeremy Roenick suffered his third severe knee injury in as many years when he collided with Anaheim center Ted Drury during the 1997 playoffs.

Jeremy Roenick

Position: **Center**
Height: **6'0"**
Weight: **170 lbs.**
Birth Date:
January 17, 1970
Birth Place: **Boston, Massachusetts**
Drafted: **1988, Chicago Blackhawks**

Left: Roenick blows past Ottawa forward Radek Bonk during a Coyote-Senators match in the 1996-97 season.

Bottom: Roenick had back-to-back 50-goal seasons for the Chicago Blackhawks in 1992 and 1993.

tion easily. Roenick is capable of stickhandling through an opponent or two, then finishing with a quick and very accurate shot. He is unpredictable, which makes him difficult to cover. Teammate Mike Gartner said, "He's a player that's capable of being a game breaker and there aren't a lot of players like that around the league."

Roenick doesn't let his relatively small stature influence his play. He likes to hit and fight for the puck along the boards. For a top center, his penalty minute totals are high, but he balances this with fine power-play work. He is so intense that each time he's on the ice, he seems to make a noticeable difference in the flow of the game.

Patrick Roy

Patrick Roy's accomplishments already place him among the NHL's all-time great goaltenders. Now, he wants to stand alone.

Roy, who passed Billy Smith's record of 88 post-season wins during the 1997 playoffs, is still young enough to reach Terry Sawchuk's NHL record of 447 regular-season wins. "I would like to pass Terry Sawchuk and I think I can," said Roy. "I'm inspired by John Vanbiesbrouck and Andy Moog. They've never

been better. I feel I can play for at least another four or five years."

As a rookie in 1985-86, Roy burst into the limelight when he led a rookie-laden Montreal squad to a surprise Stanley Cup victory. Seven years and three Vezina Trophy wins later, Roy once again carried an underdog Montreal team to a Stanley Cup triumph. During that 1993 post-season, Roy's brilliant play allowed the Canadiens to win an NHL record 10 over-

Left: Patrick Roy continues to be the NHL's greatest clutch goaltender, saving his best performances for those moments when the game is on the line.

Patrick Roy

Position: **Goaltender**
Height: **6'0"**
Weight: **192 lbs.**
Birth Date:
October 5, 1965
Birth Place:
Quebec City, Quebec
Drafted: **1984,**
Montreal Canadiens

time games. That performance earned the enigmatic goaltender his second Conn Smythe Trophy as playoff MVP.

After another fine season in 1993-94 when he led the league with seven shutouts, Roy and the Canadiens stumbled in 1994-95 and missed the play-offs. Roy finished the campaign with a losing record for the first time in his career and it appeared that he had lost his competitive edge. What he had really lost was his faith in the Canadiens' front office. Then, early in the 1995-96 campaign, he lost his composure during a 11-1 blowout loss to Detroit. That was the breaking point in an already strained relationship between the star and the front office brass. Roy demanded a trade, and he was dealt from the struggling Canadiens to Colorado, a move that would have been unimaginable months earlier when the Avalanche, previously the Quebec Nordiques, resided just down the highway from the Habs in Quebec City.

Hailed as a savior when he joined the team, Roy quickly set out to prove he was equal to the task. He was steady, though not spectacular, for the remainder of the season while he adjusted to his new surround-

Opposite top: Roy is a study in concentration as he focuses in on the action during one of his first games in an Avalanche uniform on December 13, 1995.

Opposite bottom: With Stephane Yelle and Sylvain Lefebvre providing physical support, Roy stones Florida Panthers forward Bill Lindsay during the 1996 Stanley Cup finals.

Right: Roy's lightning-quick glove hand snares a snapper off the stick of Calgary sniper Robert Reichel during a 3-2 loss to the Flames on March 12, 1997.

ings. However, once the playoffs started, he was once again a dominant force on the ice and in the dressing room. He backstopped the Avs to hard-fought series wins over Vancouver and Chicago before turning in a brilliant performance as the Avalanche upset Detroit in the semi-finals. In a four-game, final-round sweep of the Florida Panthers, his GAA was a minuscule 0.84, the third lowest mark ever recorded in a modern Stanley Cup final series. "St. Patrick" had returned to form.

It's rare for a goaltender to be a team leader, yet Roy often projects the attitude that he can't lose. "He has got a tremendous presence about him," said Colorado coach Marc Crawford. "It boosts our players' confidence as much as it deflates the confidence of the players who have to face him."

Roy's success with the butterfly style has spawned a host of imitators, but none of them use it better than he does. He is so good at blocking the lower part of the net that snipers usually have to try to beat him with perfectly-placed high shots. Roy also will challenge shooters, skating out to cut down the angle. If he finds himself out of position, he then relies upon his outstanding reflexes.

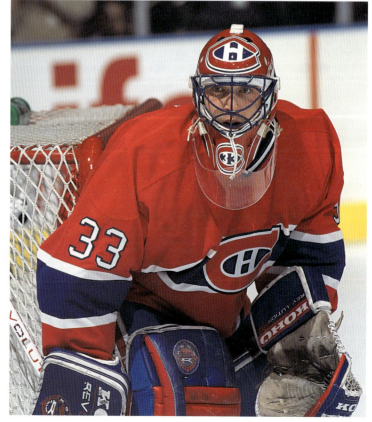

Joe Sakic

After years of waiting, Joe Sakic finally had a chance to walk into the spotlight in 1995-96, and he did so in unforgettable style. The Avalanche captain snagged the playoff MVP award and led Colorado to the Stanley Cup with a brilliant performance that ranked among the best in NHL history. However, if fans thought the shy Sakic would actually boast about his triumph, they were mistaken. Sakic remained as soft-spoken as always. He remained just as taciturn during the 1996-97 season, refusing to place blame or point fingers when he suffered a severely cut calf muscle in a collision with Eric Lindros that caused him to miss 17 games and erase any chance he had at claiming his first NHL scoring crown.

Before his Stanley Cup success in 1996, Sakic had never had a chance to play more than a handful of post-season games. Once Quebec relocated to Colorado in 1995, years of high draft picks and smart trades

Opposite top: Roy's butterfly style is perfectly pictured here as Roy and the Canadiens battle the L.A. Kings during the 1993 Stanley Cup finals.

Opposite bottom: During his glory days with the Canadiens, Roy won the Vezina Trophy three times and the Conn Smythe Trophy twice.

Right: Joe Sakic slams on the brakes to elude New York's Mark Messier as two of the game's greatest forwards face each other during the 1996-97 season.

Joe Sakic

Position: **Center**
Height: **5'11"**
Weight: **185 lbs.**
Birth Date:
July 7, 1969.
Birth Place: **Burnaby, British Columbia**
Drafted: **1987, Quebec Nordiques**

Left: Sakic attempts to slip the puck under Canuck goaltender Corey Hirsch during Colorado's 4-2 win over Vancouver on March 18, 1997.

Bottom left: Although he is known for his quiet, almost shy demeanor off the ice, Sakic can be a comic force in the dressing room.

Bottom right: When he was quietly racking up back-to-back 100-point seasons with the Quebec Nordiques, Sakic was known as "the best player that nobody knows."

made the team a Cup contender. Sakic ensured the club didn't fail in its first attempt at a championship. Utilizing his great wrist shot and snapshot, Sakic scored 18 goals, including a record six game-winners and added 16 assists in 22 playoff games.

Sakic has a style that sets him apart from other, more dazzling superstars. Former NHL player Peter McNab explained, "He's quick and explosive and he scores electrifying goals, but at the end of the game you remember someone else's goals. It's the subtleness of each of the moves."

A calculating attacker who never seems to rush a play, Sakic is constantly aware of his options, and he knows when the best moment is to pass or shoot. His passing and stickhandling skills are excellent, and his all-around ability makes him deadly on the power play. As long as he keeps shooting, he'll rank among the very best producers in the league.

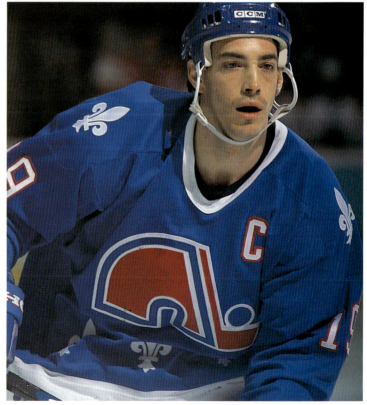

Teemu Selanne

Teemu Selanne is one attacker who frightens defensemen more than most players. The "Finnish Flash" is so gifted that he can beat an opponent in almost any manner he chooses – with his shot, his speed or his playmaking.

Although the Winnipeg Jets drafted him in 1988, Selanne stayed in Finland, developing his game while building his confidence and strength. In the 1992-93 season, Selanne shattered the rookie scoring record with 76 goals and 132 points. Previously, no rookie had scored more than 53 goals or 109 points. Injuries slowed him in the next two seasons, prompting the Jets to trade him to Anaheim in 1995-96, where he's been able to regain his stellar form. In the 1995-96

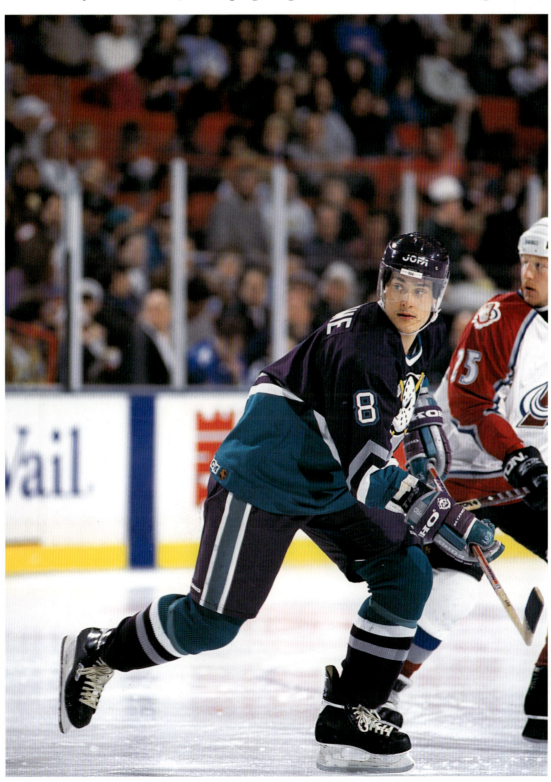

Left: Teemu Selanne was one of only two NHL players to hit the 100-point mark in 1996-97, finishing second to Mario Lemieux in the scoring race with 109 points.

Teemu Selanne

Position: **Right Wing**
Height: **6'0"**
Weight: **200 lbs.**
Birth Date:
July 3, 1970
Birth Place:
Helsinki, Finland
Drafted: **1988,**
Winnipeg Jets

Brendan Shanahan

Brendan Shanahan is the type of power forward that every winning team needs. He's a great leader, a pinpoint sniper – and he's tough.

When Shanahan first came into the NHL with the New Jersey Devils, he spent more time in the penalty box than in front of the net. His early image was that of a sharpshooting, hard-fisted banger, and the boards in the Meadowlands still bear the scars of the many opponents he plastered into the glass. His offensive skills bloomed in his third season, but his break-through came in 1993-94 in his second season with St. Louis, where he had signed as a free agent. With the Blues, he set career-highs for goals (52), assists (50), points (102) and, ironically, penalty minutes (211). Traded to Detroit early in the 1996-97 season, he has become the Red Wings' offensive motivator, leading the club in goals (47), points (88), power-play goals (20) and game-winning goals (7).

Shanahan scores most of his goals from close range with a quick, hard shot. On the power play, he uses his

Left: As he sets up in his favorite position near the opposition's crease, Brendan Shanahan prepares to make life difficult for another NHL goalie.

Opposite top: Shanahan, who tied for the league lead with 20 power-play goals in 1996-97, also finished second to Paul Kariya with 336 shots-on-goal.

Opposite bottom: In 1993-94, Shanahan became one of the few players in NHL history to score 50 goals and compile over 200 minutes in penalties in the same season.

Brendan Shanahan

Position: **Left Wing**
Height: **6'3"**
Weight: **218 lbs.**
Birth Date:
January 23, 1969
Birth Place:
Mimico, Ontario
Drafted: **1987,**
New Jersey Devils

size and strength to fend off defensemen and deflect point shots or grab rebounds. He's aggressive, persistent and he owns surprisingly soft hands.

One aspect of Shanahan's play that is sometimes overlooked is his ability to make key plays. The winger explained, "You have to be able to sense when the defining moments of a game are there. Sometimes the difference will be a hit, a fight or a goal and you have to elevate your game at that precise moment."

Known as one of the brightest, most outgoing people in the league, Shanahan also leads with his charismatic personality. He is a positive, dynamic force in the dressing room and on the ice. Once Steve Yzerman retires, Shanahan will be the logical choice as the next Detroit captain.

Above: The second player selected overall in the 1987 NHL Entry Draft, Shanahan became an instant crowd favorite at the Meadowlands with his brash hitting and deft shooting.

Left: Shanahan escapes the shadow of Flyers defenseman Mark Howe during his rookie season with the New Jersey Devils.

Scott Stevens

Scott Stevens is an ideal captain for New Jersey: he's strong-willed, hard-working and very serious. These qualities also make him one of the best and most respected defensemen in the league.

Jersey coach Jacques Lemaire, who was a dedicated player himself, observed, "There isn't one game or one practice that he doesn't give his best effort in." Since Lemaire assumed control of the team in 1993-94, Stevens has been one of his mainstays. "Every team is initially built around one player, and I thought Scott could be that player," Lemaire stated. "He had character. He had heart. He had toughness." Stevens repaid Lemaire's faith by playing superb playoff hockey as the Devils captured the Stanley Cup in 1994-95.

Left: Scott Stevens' ability to change direction while maintaining both speed and balance have made him one of the NHL's top rearguards.

Scott Stevens

Position: **Defense**
Height: **6'2"**
Weight: **210 lbs.**
Birth Date:
April 1, 1964
Birth Place:
Kitchener, Ontario
Drafted: **1982,**
Washington Capitals

A three-time All-Star, Stevens has been one of the toughest checking, hardest hitting players in the NHL since entering the league with the Washington Capitals in 1982-83. In the first half of his career, he also gained a reputation for being a fearsome fighter, but over time, he's managed to control his temper. He was once so eager to throw bodychecks that he'd take himself out of position, but he's learned to hit when the opportunity presents itself. Stevens is considered to be the best bodychecker in the NHL – he's so solidly built that many opponents just fold when he hits them. With his size and strength, he excels in the physical battles in front of his net. He is also an excellent shot-blocker. Although Stevens is no longer a big point-producer, he continues to be a physical presence on the ice and a guiding voice in the dressing room.

Mats Sundin

Mats Sundin has always had the size and skill to be an elite forward, but he never seemed to fulfill the high expectations placed on him. In 1996-97, Sundin finally put the elements of his game together, and the result was a career-rejuvenating season for the smooth-skating Swede.

A highly regarded prospect, Sundin appeared to blossom in his third NHL season when he racked up 114 points with the Quebec Nordiques. Quebec assistant general manager Gilles Leger remarked, "He's a lot like Jean Beliveau as far as size and smoothness

go. I think he can be a force in the league." However, he moved sideways for the next three seasons, scoring at a one-point-per-game pace. The results were solid, but his game was criticized for its lack of consistency and passion. Traded to Toronto in 1994, Sundin was expected to complement Doug Gilmour, but the pair never clicked on the ice and the results were evident in the standings as the Leafs spiralled towards the NHL basement.

Yet, it was while playing on a very average Maple Leaf team in 1996-97 that Sundin began to show real

Opposite top: Many pundits feel that Scott Stevens had the best defensive season of his career in 1996-97.

Opposite bottom: Stevens, seen here eating a glove from Kelly Hrudey and an elbow from Ken Morrow, has never been afraid to cause a commotion near the opposition's crease.

Right: Despite close checking from opponents like Al MacInnis, Mats Sundin still finished seventh in league scoring with 41 goals and 94 points.

Mats Sundin

Position:
Center/Right Wing
Height: **6'4"**
Weight: **215 lbs.**
Birth Date:
February 13, 1971
Birth Place:
Bromma, Sweden
Drafted: **1989,**
Quebec Nordiques

leadership capabilities. As captain Gilmour's game began to wane, Sundin picked up the offensive slack and returned to the form that he flashed so brilliantly in 1992-93. Night after night, he was the best Maple Leaf player on the ice and the results are evident in the statistics: Sundin led the Leafs in seven different offensive categories in 1996-97 including goals (41), assists (53), and points (94), and became the only Maple Leaf player other than Gilmour and Dave Andreychuk to finish among the NHL's top ten scorers in the past 16 years.

Sundin's improvement stemmed from an off-season training program that increased his strength and conditioning. Combined with his natural size, this produced a forward who could bull through checkers or skate rings around them for three periods. Sundin's skating is a big asset – he has a long stride that few can match, and he's quick. He has a superb, well-rounded collection of shots, including the NHL's best backhand, a weapon that can take any netminder by surprise. Sundin is more of a finisher than a playmaker, and he has the potential to be a consistent 50-goal scorer.

Keith Tkachuk

Not many players become team captain in their second NHL season, but then again, Keith Tkachuk is no ordinary player. Described as "insanely intense" by Ron Wilson, who coached him during the 1996 World Cup Tournament, Tkachuk has been the heart of the Winnipeg/Phoenix franchise since he donned the captain's "C" in 1993-94.

Perhaps one of the reasons he seems wise beyond his years is that he has already travelled a difficult road during his first few seasons in the NHL. In 1995-96, Tkachuk was declared a free agent and he signed an offer sheet with the Chicago Blackhawks. The Jets matched the Chicago offer and were able retain the rights to their rising star, but there was acrimony in the front office over Tkachuk's attempted defection. In 1995-96, Winnipeg coach Terry Simpson took away Tkachuk's captaincy, but instead of brooding, Tkachuk blistered the opposition, leading his club in goals (50), points (98), plus/minus (+11), power play goals (20), game-winning goals (6) and shots (249). When the club moved to Phoenix to begin the 1996-97 season, new coach Don Hay returned the "C" to Tkachuk's chest, and the wily Coyote has re-established himself as the team leader. He led the Coyotes in scoring in 1996-97 with 86 points and led the NHL with 52 goals, despite scoring only four goals in his first 19 games.

Tkachuk is one of the toughest and most hot-tempered players in the league, which is both an asset and a detriment. He may take the occasional bad penalty, but he also can dominate in battles for the puck. The fear he inspires in opponents and the will to win he exhibits always help the Coyotes. In this way, he is like a young Mark Messier.

Considering he is such a physical player, Tkachuk has surprisingly good finesse. Bobby Smith, Phoenix executive vice-president of hockey operations, said, "I've seen him score beautiful goals, make outstanding plays. His hands really are terrific." Tkachuk responded, "I've never really considered myself a goal-scorer. I'm not sure I do now. I'm just trying to keep it simple, go to the net and sacrifice my body."

After gaining a wild reputation, Tkachuk has matured off the ice, but he'll never be calm on it and that should drive Coyote fans wild.

Left: Keith Tkachuk came of age during the 1996-97 season, winning his first goal-scoring crown by snapping 52 pucks into enemy nets during the season.

Keith Tkachuk

Position: **Left Wing**
Height: **6'2"**
Weight: **210 lbs.**
Birth Date:
March 28, 1972
Birth Place: **Melrose, Massachusetts**
Drafted: **1990, Winnipeg Jets**

John Vanbiesbrouck

Although John Vanbiesbrouck won the Vezina Trophy in 1985-86, he did not firmly establish himself as an elite goalie until he joined the Florida Panthers in 1993-94. Now, most insiders would rank this fiery competitor among the NHL's top five goalies.

Early in his career, "The Beezer" was troubled by inconsistency. When he was confident, he played very aggressively, challenging shooters, but when he was down on himself, he could allow bad goals. Now that he's satisfied with his role in Florida and the team around him, he's more consistent than ever.

"His play gives his teammates an enormous sense of confidence," said Philadelphia coach Terry Murray. "They can be aggressive. They can take chances because they are so confident Vanbiesbrouck will be there for them."

While his first three seasons in Florida were excellent, Vanbiesbrouck couldn't shake the criticism that he wasn't a big-game goalie, since he had only 13 postseason wins to his credit. In 1995-96, Vanbiesbrouck dismissed his doubters by leading Florida to the Stanley Cup finals. It marked only the second time

Left: When the Florida Panthers decide to "leave it to Beezer," John Vanbiesbrouck usually comes up with the saves to ensure another victory for the "rat-pack."

Opposite top: In 1985-86, Vanbiesbrouck recorded a career-high 31 wins in helping the NY Rangers advance to the Conference Championship finals.

Opposite bottom: Although the Panthers' 1997 playoff run was derailed by the NY Rangers, Vanbiesbrouck had a marvellous regular season with a career-best goals-against average of 2.29 and a franchise-high 27 victories.

John Vanbiesbrouck

Position: **Goaltender**
Height: **5'8"**
Weight: **176 lbs.**
Birth Date:
September 4, 1963
Birth Place:
Detroit, Michigan
Drafted: **1981,**
New York Rangers

since 1926 that a team appearing in the playoffs for the first time went all the way to the championship round. Although the Panthers were swept out of the finals by the surging Colorado Avalanche, Vanbiesbrouck won a career-high 12 playoff games and compiled a 2.25 goals-against average in 22 post-season matches.

Vanbiesbrouck has many strengths: he's quick, he's a good skater, his glove hand is very good and he utilizes his stick as well as anyone. His positioning is sound and he rarely allows a bad-angle goal. He benefits from playing on a defensive team, but the team also benefits from him. At no time was this clearer than during the 1996-97 season. Although the Panthers were hurt by injuries, Vanbiesbrouck continued to provide his team with top-notch goaltending, and he ended up winning a franchise-high 27 games.

Alexei Yashin

An enigma during much of his early NHL career, Alexei Yashin seems moody at times, upbeat and jovial at others. When he was criticized for using the media as a bargaining tool during his contract disputes with the Ottawa Senators, he decided to let his talent do the talking, and the Senators have benefitted from Yashin's decision to focus on his on-ice progress.

After a 79-point rookie campaign, a combination of injury and contract squabbles slowed his development. While it was clear that the big Russian had a talent for scoring highlight-reel goals and an abundance of undeveloped potential, it wasn't until the 1996-97 season that he had a opportunity to prove himself in the pressure-cooker of the playoff race. He led the Ottawa Senators in goals (35), points (75), game-winning goals (5) and shots-on-goal (291) during the 1996-97 season as he led the Senators to their first playoff berth in modern franchise history.

Yashin's greatest skill is his one-on-one play. He can stickhandle through several opponents and finish the play with a superb shot. He doesn't apply himself consistently, however, and he doesn't use his linemates enough. One area he has improved is his leadership. In 1996-97, teammate Steve Duchesne said, "He's getting more involved in the dressing room now. He's speaking up. It's a different Yash now and everybody loves it." As the Senators become a competitive team, Yashin will be expected to do more of this.

Left: Alexei Yashin and his Ottawa teammates, who made it to the post-season for the first time in franchise history in 1996-97, took the Buffalo Sabres to overtime in the seventh game before a goal by Sabres forward Derek Plante ended the Senators' Cinderella season.

Alexei Yashin

Position: **Center**
Height: **6'3"**
Weight: **215 lbs.**
Birth Date:
November 5, 1973
Birth Place:
Sverdlovsk, USSR
Drafted: **1992,
Ottawa Senators**

Steve Yzerman

In an era dominated by great offensive centers, Steve Yzerman ranks as one of the best. Gretzky, Messier and Lemieux may have prevented him from winning any major NHL honors, but the sold-out crowds at Detroit's Joe Louis Arena leave no doubt as to who their favorite star in Motown is. Before he joined the Red Wings in 1983-84, Detroit had missed the playoffs in 15 of the previous 17 seasons. Since Yzerman arrived, the team has only missed the playoffs twice and has finished first in its division six times. It's no wonder he's called a wonder.

Early in his career, Yzerman's individual success far exceeded that of his team. Former Detroit coach Jacques Demers recalled, "On many nights, this young man carried the team on his shoulders. He could not accept that the team was the worst in hockey. I can't remember a night when he didn't come to play." Those qualities brought Yzerman the distinction of being named the youngest captain in NHL history when Detroit gave him the "C" in 1986.

In 1987-88, that promotion provided motivation and Yzerman went from very good to great, scoring 50 goals in 64 games and reaching the 100-point mark for the first of six consecutive years. In 1988-89, he was simply fabulous, recording 155 points and winning the Lester Pearson Award as the NHL's outstanding player as voted by the players themselves.

Yzerman has taken his share of the blame for

Left: One of the NHL's top face-off men, Steve Yzerman prepares to take another key draw against Colorado center Stephane Yelle during a confrontation between two of the NHL's top teams.

Steve Yzerman

Position: **Center**
Height: **5'11"**
Weight: **185 lbs.**
Birth Date:
May 9, 1965
Birth Place: **Cranbrook, British Columbia**
Drafted: **1983, Detroit Red Wings**

Left: In 1996-97, Yzerman led the Red Wings in assists for the 10th time in 14 seasons, setting up his teammates 63 times during the season.

Below: Steve Yzerman was only 21 years old when he was appointed captain of the Red Wings prior to the 1986-87 season. The 1997-98 campaign marks his 12th season as the Detroit captain, tying him with former Maple Leafs' great George Armstrong as the longest-serving captain in NHL history.

Opposite: Yzerman reached another career milestone when he played his 1000th regular-season game on February 19, 1997.

Detroit's post-season failures in the 1990's, but those charges are unfounded, according to many of his peers. "Steve wants to win in the worst way," said Rangers coach Colin Campbell, "but he has never been the kind of guy to break his stick or trash a hallway to show his competitiveness."

The one word that describes Yzerman's style is effortless. He is a fluid, balanced skater who can make any move: sharp turns, sudden stops, quick accelerations. He sees the ice very well and makes excellent passes. Yzerman has a host of dekes and fakes that make him deadly on breakaways or one-on-one situations. His goal-scoring has dropped since his prime, but he still has a fine wrist shot.

Remarkably, Yzerman has turned from a one-way player into a dedicated two-way performer in the last few seasons, an unselfish act that perfectly describes his devotion to his team. He was rewarded for that dedication with a long-term contract that will keep him in a Red Wings uniform for the remainder of his career.

Index

Acknowledgments

The publisher would like to thank the following individuals who helped with the preparation of this book: Jean Martin, the editor and picture researcher; David Eldred, the designer; and Elizabeth McCarthy, the indexer.

Picture Credits
Allsport USA: N. Butler: 76; G. Cratty: 1, 57(top), 88(bottom), 94(bottom left), 104(bottom); E. Hasch: 88(top); J. Patronite: 56; D. Pensinger: 8(top), 47(top); M. Powell: 43; N. Reid: 3, 22(bottom), 94(top); R. Stewart: 70, 90(top); M. Stookman: 50.
Bruce Bennett Studios: 24, 26-27, 27, 28, 41, 49(bottom), 102(bottom), 105; C. Anderson: 6(right), 45, 60, 86(bottom), 89, 103; B. Bennett: 9(right), 11, 15(top), 21, 29(top), 30, 33, 36(both), 39(both), 40, 52(bottom), 53, 59(bottom), 62, 64, 68, 77(bottom), 81(bottom), 92(top), 93; T. Biegun: 32, 97; M. Desjardins: 71; M. DiGiacomo: 12(top); M. DiGirolamo: 17(bottom), 46, 47(bottom), 100(top), 102(top); H. DiRocco: 57(bottom), 58; A. Foxall: 23, 31(top), 42(both), 48, 63(top), 80, 82, 96, 110(top); J. Giamundo: 8(bottom), 17(top), 18, 19(both), 41(top), 54(top), 61, 73, 74, 77(bottom), 81(top), 85, 95, 99(top), 107(top); M. Hicks: 52(top), 104(top), 109, 110(bottom); R. Laberge: 34, 35(bottom), 51, 55, 63(bottom), 94(bottom right), 111; S. Levy: 6(left), 12(bottom), 16; R. Lewis: 107(bottom); J. McIsaac: 4, 7(both), 10, 13, 14, 15(bottom), 25, 29(bottom), 37, 41(bottom), 49(top), 69, 101; J. Michaud: 108; B. Miller: 100(bottom); A. Pichette: 87; W. Roberts: 72; H. Scull, Jr.: 79, 106; J. Tremmel: 9(left), 38; B. Winkler: 20, 22(top), 92(bottom), 98, 99(bottom); B. Wippert: 54(bottom).
Hockey Hall of Fame and Museum, Toronto: 67(top), 84(top).
Reuters/Archive Photos: M. Blake: 2, 59(top), 65(top), 78, 86(top); J. Christensen: 75; G. Caskey: 90(bottom); A. Clark: 84(bottom); S. Gross: 65(bottom); R. Williamson: 35(top), 91; J. Wolke: 31(bottom).